Overcoming Common Problems Series

Coping with Hearing Loss
Christine Craggs-Hinton

Coping with Heartburn and Reflux
Dr Tom Smith

Coping with Kidney Disease
Dr Tom Smith

Coping with Life after Stroke
Dr Mareeni Raymond

Coping with Macular Degeneration
Dr Patricia Gilbert

Coping with a Mid-life Crisis
Derek Milne

Coping with PMS
Dr Farah Ahmed and Dr Emma Cordle

Coping with Polycystic Ovary Syndrome
Christine Craggs-Hinton

Coping with Postnatal Depression
Sandra L. Wheatley

Coping with Radiotherapy
Dr Terry Priestman

Coping with a Stressed Nervous System
Dr Kenneth Hambly and Alice Muir

Coping with Suicide
Maggie Helen

Coping with Tinnitus
Christine Craggs-Hinton

Coping with Type 2 Diabetes
Susan Elliot-Wright

Coping with Your Partner's Death: Your bereavement guide
Geoff Billings

The Depression Diet Book
Theresa Cheung

Depression: Healing emotional distress
Linda Hurcombe

Depressive Illness
Dr Tim Cantopher

Eating for a Healthy Heart
Robert Povey, Jacqui Morrell and Rachel Povey

Every Woman's Guide to Digestive Health
Jill Eckersley

The Fertility Handbook
Dr Philippa Kaye

The Fibromyalgia Healing Diet
Christine Craggs-Hinton

Free Your Life from Fear
Jenny Hare

Free Yourself from Depression
Colin and Margaret Sutherland

A Guide to Anger Management
Mary Hartley

Heal the Hurt: How to forgive and move o
Dr Ann Macaskill

Helping Children Cope with Anxiety
Jill Eckersley

Helping Children Cope with Grief
Rosemary Wells

How to Approach Death
Julia Tugendhat

How to be a Healthy Weight
Philippa Pigache

How to Beat Pain
Christine Craggs-Hinton

How to Cope with Difficult People
Alan Houel and Christian Godefroy

How to Fight Chronic Fatigue
Christine Craggs-Hinton

How to Get the Best from Your Doctor
Dr Tom Smith

How to Stop Worrying
Dr Frank Tallis

How to Talk to Your Child
Penny Oates

Hysterectomy: Is it right for you?
Janet Wright

The IBS Healing Plan
Theresa Cheung

Letting Go of Anxiety and Depression
Dr Windy Dryden

Living with Angina
Dr Tom Smith

Living with Asperger Syndrome
Dr Joan Gomez

Living with Autism
Fiona Marshall

Living with Bipolar Disorder
Dr Neel Burton

Living with Birthmarks and Blemishes
Gordon Lamont

Living with Crohn's Disease
Dr Joan Gomez

Living with Eczema
Jill Eckersley

Living with Fibromyalgia
Christine Craggs-Hinton

Living with Food Intolerance
Alex Gazzola

Overcoming Common Problems Series

Living with Gluten Intolerance
Jane Feinmann

Living with Grief
Dr Tony Lake

Living with Loss and Grief
Julia Tugendhat

Living with Osteoarthritis
Dr Patricia Gilbert

Living with Osteoporosis
Dr Joan Gomez

Living with Physical Disability and Amputation
Dr Keren Fisher

Living with Rheumatoid Arthritis
Philippa Pigache

Living with Schizophrenia
Dr Neel Burton and Dr Phil Davison

Living with a Seriously Ill Child
Dr Jan Aldridge

Living with Sjögren's Syndrome
Sue Dyson

Living with Type 1 Diabetes
Dr Tom Smith

Losing a Child
Linda Hurcombe

The Multiple Sclerosis Diet Book
Tessa Buckley

Osteoporosis: Prevent and treat
Dr Tom Smith

Overcome Your Fear of Flying
Professor Robert Bor, Dr Carina Eriksen and
Margaret Oakes

Overcoming Agoraphobia
Melissa Murphy

Overcoming Anorexia
Professor J. Hubert Lacey, Christine Craggs-Hinton
and Kate Robinson

Overcoming Anxiety
Dr Windy Dryden

Overcoming Back Pain
Dr Tom Smith

Overcoming Depression
Dr Windy Dryden and Sarah Opie

Overcoming Emotional Abuse
Susan Elliot-Wright

Overcoming Hurt
Dr Windy Dryden

Overcoming Insomnia
Susan Elliot-Wright

Overcoming Jealousy
Dr Windy Dryden

Overcoming Panic and Related Anxiety Disorders
Margaret Hawkins

Overcoming Procrastination
Dr Windy Dryden

Overcoming Shyness and Social Anxiety
Ruth Searle

Overcoming Tiredness and Exhaustion
Fiona Marshall

Reducing Your Risk of Cancer
Dr Terry Priestman

Safe Dieting for Teens
Linda Ojeda

Self-discipline: How to get it and how to keep it
Dr Windy Dryden

The Self-Esteem Journal
Alison Waines

Simplify Your Life
Naomi Saunders

Sinusitis: Steps to healing
Dr Paul Carson

Stammering: Advice for all ages
Renée Byrne and Louise Wright

Stress-related Illness
Dr Tim Cantopher

Ten Steps to Positive Living
Dr Windy Dryden

Think Your Way to Happiness
Dr Windy Dryden and Jack Gordon

The Thinking Person's Guide to Happiness
Ruth Searle

Tranquillizers and Antidepressants: When to take them, how to stop
Professor Malcolm Lader

The Traveller's Good Health Guide
Dr Ted Lankester

Treating Arthritis Diet Book
Margaret Hills

Treating Arthritis: The drug-free way
Margaret Hills and Christine Horner

Treating Arthritis: More ways to a drug-free life
Margaret Hills

Understanding Obsessions and Compulsions
Dr Frank Tallis

When Someone You Love Has Dementia
Susan Elliot-Wright

When Someone You Love Has Depression
Barbara Baker

Overcoming Common Problems Series

Selected titles

A full list of titles is available from Sheldon Press,
36 Causton Street, London SW1P 4ST and on our website at
www.sheldonpress.co.uk

The Assertiveness Handbook
Mary Hartley

Assertiveness: Step by step
Dr Windy Dryden and Daniel Constantinou

Backache: What you need to know
Dr David Delvin

Body Language: What you need to know
David Cohen

The Cancer Survivor's Handbook
Dr Terry Priestman

The Candida Diet Book
Karen Brody

The Chronic Fatigue Healing Diet
Christine Craggs-Hinton

The Chronic Pain Diet Book
Neville Shone

Cider Vinegar
Margaret Hills

The Complete Carer's Guide
Bridget McCall

The Confidence Book
Gordon Lamont

Confidence Works
Gladeana McMahon

Coping Successfully with Pain
Neville Shone

Coping Successfully with Panic Attacks
Shirley Trickett

Coping Successfully with Period Problems
Mary-Claire Mason

Coping Successfully with Psoriasis
Christine Craggs-Hinton

Coping Successfully with Ulcerative Colitis
Peter Cartwright

Coping Successfully with Varicose Veins
Christine Craggs-Hinton

Coping Successfully with Your Hiatus Hernia
Dr Tom Smith

Coping Successfully with Your Irritable Bowel
Rosemary Nicol

Coping When Your Child Has Cerebral Palsy
Jill Eckersley

Coping with Age-related Memory Loss
Dr Tom Smith

Coping with Birth Trauma and Postnatal Depression
Lucy Jolin

Coping with Bowel Cancer
Dr Tom Smith

Coping with Candida
Shirley Trickett

Coping with Chemotherapy
Dr Terry Priestman

Coping with Chronic Fatigue
Trudie Chalder

Coping with Coeliac Disease
Karen Brody

Coping with Compulsive Eating
Ruth Searle

Coping with Diabetes in Childhood and Adolescence
Dr Philippa Kaye

Coping with Diverticulitis
Peter Cartwright

Coping with Down's Syndrome
Fiona Marshall

Coping with Dyspraxia
Jill Eckersley

Coping with Eating Disorders and Body Image
Christine Craggs-Hinton

Coping with Epilepsy in Children and Young People
Susan Elliot-Wright

Coping with Family Stress
Dr Peter Cheevers

Coping with Gout
Christine Craggs-Hinton

Coping with Hay Fever
Christine Craggs-Hinton

Coping with Headaches and Migraine
Alison Frith

Coping with Life's Challenges

DR WINDY DRYDEN was born in London in 1950. He has worked in psychotherapy and counselling for over 30 years, d is th author or editor of over 170 books, including *How to Accept Yc If h don Press, 1999)* and *Self-discipline: How to get it and how to keep Press, 2009).* Dr Dryden is Professor of Psychotherapeutic Stuc hs, University of London.

Overcoming Common Problems

Coping with Life's Challenges
Moving on from adversity

DR WINDY DRYDEN

First published in Great Britain in 2010

Sheldon Press
36 Causton Street
London SW1P 4ST

British Library Cataloguing-in-Publication Data
A catalogue record for this book is available from the British Library

ISBN 978–1–84709–098–0

1 3 5 7 9 10 8 6 4 2

Typeset by Fakenham Photosetting Ltd, Fakenham, Norfolk
Printed in Great Britain by Ashford Colour Press

Produced on paper from sustainable forests

Contents

Preface   ix

1   Cognitive Behavioural Therapy and what it has to offer   1
2   Dealing with personal limitations   17
3   Dealing with loss   32
4   Dealing with uncertainty   45
5   Dealing with lack of control   59
6   Dealing with failure   74
7   Dealing with disapproval and rejection   86
8   Dealing with unfairness, injustice and betrayal   98

Index   115

Preface

In this book, I will consider some of the most common but difficult challenges that life poses for us. As in my other books for Sheldon Press, my focus will be on how we disturb ourselves about these adversities and what we can do to effectively address our unconstructive responses so that we can move on with our lives as healthily as we can. In doing so, I will draw upon insights derived from Cognitive Behaviour Therapy (CBT) which I have practised for over 30 years.

It would be nice to live a charmed life, but who among us does not have personal limitations to put up with, losses to come to terms with, uncertainties to cope with, areas in life where we are not in control, failures to deal with, people who disapprove of and reject us and times when we have been betrayed and treated unfairly and unjustly? My guess is that the answer to this question is 'Very few.'

These are the very challenges that I will discuss in this book, so you could say that all human life is in within its pages!

Windy Dryden
London and Eastbourne

1

Cognitive Behavioural Therapy and what it has to offer

Introduction

This book is based on ideas that stem from a tradition in counselling and psychotherapy known as Cognitive Behavioural Therapy (CBT). This tradition has received much attention in the popular and professional press since it is the one that is most frequently recommended for a variety of psychological problems by the National Institute for Health and Clinical Excellence (NICE), whose task is to recommend treatments (both medical and psychological) that have been shown by research to be effective. Thus, CBT has good research credentials when it comes to the topics that I discuss in this book.

But what are my credentials for writing the book? Well, I first trained in CBT in 1977 and was one of the first British therapists to do so, and I have been practising it for over 30 years in a variety of clinical contexts. I have written widely in the field and specialize in bringing the insights of CBT to the general public through my self-help books for Sheldon Press. Also, much of what I write here is based on my clinical experience. While most of the examples that I discuss in this book come from my casebook, please note that they have been heavily disguised to protect the confidentiality of those involved.

Having established the credentials of CBT as the foundation of this book and of myself as its author, let me now discuss what CBT is and what it has to offer you as you grapple with the adversities that life can throw at you.

CBT in a nutshell

Cognitive Behavioural Therapy (CBT) is a therapeutic tradition that focuses particularly on how we think and how we behave in understanding whether we respond healthily or unhealthily to life's adversities. It is a tradition that was founded by two Americans working separately in the 1950s: Dr Albert Ellis, the originator of the first CBT approach, known as Rational Emotive Behaviour Therapy, and Dr

1

Aaron Beck, the originator of Cognitive Therapy, perhaps the most practised form of CBT today. This book is based on both approaches and on the work of others in the CBT tradition.

However, while CBT in its present form dates from the 1950s, it has its roots in Stoic philosophy and in particular the writings of Epictetus (AD 55–135) whose frequently quoted statement defines the heart of CBT: 'People are disturbed not by things, but by the views which they take of them.' Let's take a closer look at the major principles of CBT.

The ABCs of CBT

CBT employs an ABC model to help people understand how we disturb ourselves about life's adversities. Let me put Epictetus' dictum, presented above, into the ABC framework before I explain this model in more detail:

A = Things
B = View
C = Disturbance

There are a number of approaches in the CBT tradition and each one uses the ABC model in a slightly different way. As this book is most closely associated with a CBT approach devised by Dr Albert Ellis, known as Rational Emotive Behaviour Therapy (REBT), I will present REBT's ABC model here:

A = Adversity
B = Belief
C = Consequences of the belief about 'A'

Let me discuss the ABC elements in turn, beginning with 'B' (beliefs), which is the heart of CBT.

'B' stands for beliefs: the heart of CBT

As Epictetus noted all those years ago, the beliefs that we hold about events largely determine how we respond to these events. This in my opinion is the heart of CBT. Albert Ellis, the founder of REBT, argued further that the rationality of the beliefs that we hold has a crucial effect on the healthiness of our responses. Let's consider this more closely.

Irrational beliefs underpin unhealthy responses

Albert Ellis argued that irrational beliefs about life's adversities underpin our unhealthy emotional and behavioural responses to these adversities. Here is what Ellis meant by an irrational belief:

An irrational belief is:

- rigid or extreme;
- false;
- illogical;
- largely unproductive in its emotional and behavioural consequences.

Ellis listed four major irrational beliefs:

1 *A rigid demand* When we hold a rigid demand we focus on what we want or don't want in a given situation and then we make this desire rigid by demanding that we must get what we want or that we must not get what we don't want.

2 *An awfulizing belief* When we hold an awfulizing belief, we acknowledge that it is bad when our desires are not met, and then we make this extreme by saying that it is awful or the end of the world when we don't get what we want or when we get what we don't want.

3 *A low frustration tolerance (LFT) belief* When we hold an LFT belief, we hold the extreme idea that it is unbearable when our desires are not met.

4 *A depreciation belief* When we hold a depreciation belief about ourselves, others and/or life conditions, the following is the case:
   (a) We depreciate ourselves when we hold ourselves responsible for the adversity that has befallen us.
   (b) We depreciate others when we consider that they are responsible for the adversity that has befallen us.
   (c) We depreciate life conditions when we consider that these are responsible for the adversity that has befallen us.

Rational beliefs underpin healthy responses

Albert Ellis argued that rational beliefs about life's adversities underpin our healthy emotional and behavioural responses to these adversities. Here is what Ellis meant by a rational belief:

> *A rational belief is:*
> - flexible or non-extreme;
> - true;
> - logical;
> - largely productive in its emotional and behavioural consequences.

Ellis listed four major rational beliefs:

1 *A non-dogmatic preference* When we hold a non-dogmatic preference rigid demand, we focus on what we want or don't want in a given situation and then we keep this desire flexible by acknowledging that we don't have to get what we want, or that we don't have to be spared getting what we don't want.

2 *A non-awfulizing belief* When we hold a non-awfulizing belief, we acknowledge that it is bad when our desires are not met and then we make this non-extreme by saying that it is not awful or the end of the world when we don't get what we want, or when we get what we don't want.

3 *A high frustration tolerance (HFT) belief* When we hold an HFT belief, we hold the non-extreme idea that while it may be difficult to put up with the situation where our desires are not met, this is not unbearable and it is worth bearing.

4 *An acceptance belief* When we hold an acceptance belief about ourselves, others and/or life conditions, the following is the case:
   (a) We accept ourselves when we hold ourselves responsible for the adversity that has befallen us.
   (b) We accept others when we consider that they are responsible for the adversity that has befallen us.
   (c) We accept life conditions when we consider that these are responsible for the adversity that has befallen us.

'A' stands for adversity

Because of the nature of this book, I will refer to 'A' as an adversity which is a significantly negative life event. However, when Albert Ellis first introduced his version of the ABC model, 'A' stood for 'activating event'. This was the event that activated the person's beliefs that explained his or her response to the event in question. In this model, 'A' could be something that actually happened (an actual event) or it could be something that the person thought had happened (an inferred event) and which may or may not have happened.

Here is an example. Two people, Bill and Ben, were work colleagues, doing the same job at a factory. Their employer announced that 30 per cent of the workforce would be made redundant, and both Bill had Ben were duly selected. Thus, they were both exposed to the same actual event (i.e. redundancy). However, while Bill had a response to the redundancy itself ('A' = actual event), Ben's response was to his inference that he was made redundant because his employer thought he was useless ('A' = inferred event). This inferred event is a hunch about the actual event which may or may not be true, but which Ben thinks is true and reacts to accordingly. When 'A's are inferred events, they do need to be tested against the available information, but this is best done when the person is not disturbed about 'A'. If this is the case, he or she needs to accept that disturbance and then investigate 'A'. For this reason, if Ben was disturbed about his inferred 'A', he would be advised to assume temporarily that this 'A' was true (i.e. that his employers made him redundant because they did think he was useless), and then to identify, examine and change his irrational belief so that he can re-examine the accuracy of his 'A' when he is no longer disturbed about it.

Let me summarize Bill and Ben's ABCs about being made redundant, where their 'A's are different.

Bill's ABC

> A (Actual event) = 'I was made redundant'
> B = Belief about being made redundant
> C = Consequence of the belief about being made redundant

Ben's ABC

> A (Inferred event) = 'They made me redundant because they
>   think I am useless'
> B = Belief about being thought useless
> C = Consequence of the belief about being thought useless

In this book, I will be discussing how to respond healthily to some of life's most challenging adversities at 'A'. You may think that people will generally disturb themselves about the actual adversities. However, my clinical experience over the years has taught me not to make this assumption. Rather, it often happens, as with Ben's case, that even in the face of very challenging adversities, people may disturb themselves about features of the situation which may not be an integral part of the situation at all. Thus, when Ben was made redundant, he disturbed himself about being thought of as useless rather than about the fact of his redundancy.

So as you read the subsequent chapters it is important that you remember that people may disturb themselves about life's actual adversities, or about subjective aspects of these adversities, or both. I will discuss this issue throughout the rest of this book.

'C' stands for the consequences of the belief about the adversity

There are three major consequences of holding beliefs about life's adversities. These consequences are emotional, behavioural and thinking in nature. Although in reality these consequences are interrelated, I will discuss them separately here.

Emotional consequences

By definition, an adversity is a negative event, and therefore it is quite appropriate, and indeed healthy, for you to have negative emotions if you experience such an adversity. Yes, that's right – negative emotions can be healthy. CBT and, in particular, REBT distinguish between emotions that are negative in feeling tone but healthy in effects, and emotions that are negative in feeling tone but unhealthy in effects. The former are known as healthy negative emotions (HNEs) and help you move on when you encounter a life challenge, while the latter are known as unhealthy negative emotions (UNEs), and when you experience these feelings you tend to get stuck or bogged down and don't move on.

According to CBT, unhealthy negative emotions largely stem from irrational beliefs about life's adversities, while healthy negative emotions stem largely from rational beliefs about these same adversities.

In Table 1, I present a list of common adversities and list the unhealthy negative emotions and healthy negative emotions (in that order) that are most often experienced about each adversity.

When reading the above list of negative emotions, it is important to realize that we do not have commonly agreed words in the English language to describe healthy negative emotions. The terms that I have used on the right represent my own attempt to denote HNEs. Feel free to use alternative terms that are more meaningful to you.

Table 1 Common adversities and their associated emotions

Adversity	Unhealthy negative emotions (UNEs) vs healthy negative emotions (HNEs)
Threat	Anxiety vs concern
Loss or failure	Depression vs sadness
Breaking your moral code; failing to live up to your moral code; hurting someone	Guilt vs remorse
Falling far short of your ideal in a social context	Shame vs disappointment
Being betrayed or let down by someone, and thinking you do not deserve such treatment	Hurt vs sorrow
A personal rule being transgressed by yourself or another; another threatening your self-esteem; frustration	Unhealthy anger vs healthy anger
Threat to valued relationship	Unhealthy jealousy vs healthy jealousy
Others having what you value and lack	Unhealthy envy vs healthy envy

Behavioural consequences

When you hold a belief about an adversity, you act in a certain way or have an urge to act in a certain way but don't act on the urge. This latter is called an action tendency in CBT.

According to CBT, unconstructive behaviour and action tendencies largely stem from irrational beliefs about life's adversities, while constructive behaviour and action tendencies stem largely from rational beliefs about these same adversities.

In Table 2, I present a list of unhealthy negative emotions and healthy negative emotions (in that order) and the most common behaviours and action tendencies associated with each.

Table 2 Negative emotions and associated behaviours and action tendencies

Unhealthy negative emotion with associated unconstructive behaviours and action tendencies	Healthy negative emotion with associated constructive behaviours and action tendencies
Anxiety	Concern
• Withdrawing from threat	• Confronting threat
• Avoiding threat	• Seeking reassurance when reassurable
• Seeking reassurance even though not reassurable	
• Seeking safety from threat	
Depression	Sadness
• Prolonged withdrawal from enjoyable activities	• Engaging with enjoyable activities after a period of mourning or adjustment to the loss
Guilt	Remorse
• Begging for forgiveness	• Asking, not begging, for forgiveness
Shame	Disappointment
• Withdrawing from others	• Keeping in contact with others
• Avoiding eye contact with others	• Maintaining eye contact with others
Hurt	Sorrow
• Sulking	• Assertion and communicating with others
Unhealthy anger	Healthy anger
• Aggression (direct and indirect)	• Assertion
Unhealthy jealousy	Healthy jealousy
• Prolonged suspicious questioning of the other person	• Brief, open-minded questioning of the other person
• Checking on the other	• Not checking on the other
• Restricting the other	• Not restricting the other
Unhealthy envy	Healthy envy
• Spoiling the other's enjoyment of the desired possession	• Striving to gain a similar possession for yourself if it is truly what you want

Thinking consequences

So far we have seen that beliefs have an impact on the way we feel about an adversity and act in response to it. In addition, our beliefs have an impact on the inferences we make about what we encounter in life and the rules that we construct about ourselves, others and life conditions. Thus, when our beliefs are irrational (i.e. rigid and/or extreme) then our subsequent thinking is likely to be grossly distorted and skewed in a negative direction. However, when our beliefs are rational (i.e. flexible and/or non-extreme), our subsequent thinking is likely to be balanced and realistic.

In Table 3, I present and illustrate some of the major thinking distortions put forward by cognitive therapists and show how they stem from irrational beliefs. I then present the alternative rational beliefs and show how they lead to more realistic and balanced thinking. In the examples provided, the thinking distortion and realistic alternative are in italics.

Table 3 Major thinking distortions and rational alternative beliefs

Thinking distortion and realistic alternative	Illustration
Jumping to unwarranted conclusions (When something bad happens, you make a negative interpretation and treat this as a fact even though there is no definite evidence that convincingly supports your conclusions)	'Since they have seen me badly fail, as I absolutely should not have done, *they will view me as an incompetent worm.*'
Sticking to the facts and testing out your hunches (When something bad happens, you stick to the facts and resolve to test out any negative interpretations you may make, which you view as hunches to be examined rather than as facts)	'Since they have seen me fail as I would have preferred not to do, but do not demand that I absolutely should not have done, I am not sure how they will view me. *I think that some will think badly of me, others will be compassionate towards me and yet others may not have noticed or will be neutral about my failure. I can always ask them, if I want to know.*'
All-or-none thinking (The use of black-and-white categories)	'I must not fail at any important task, *and if I do, I will only ever fail again.*'
Multi-category thinking (The use of many relevant categories)	'I would like not to fail at any important task, but this does not mean that I must not do so. *If I do fail, I may well succeed and fail at important tasks in the future.*'

Thinking distortion and realistic alternative	Illustration
Overgeneralization (When something bad happens, making a generalization from this experience that goes far beyond the data at hand)	'My boss must like me *and if he or she does not, nobody at work will like me.*'
Making a realistic generalization (When something goes wrong, making a generalization from this experience that is warranted by the data at hand)	'I want my boss to like me, but he or she does not have to do so. *If my boss does not like me, it follows that others at work may or may not like me.*'
Focusing on the negative (You pick out a single negative detail and dwell on it exclusively so that your vision of all reality becomes darkened, like the drop of ink that discolours the entire glass of water)	'Because I can't stand things going wrong, as they must not, *I can't see any good that is happening in my life.*'
Focusing on the complexity of experiences (You focus on a negative detail, but integrate this detail into the complexity of positive, negative and neutral features of life)	'I would prefer it if things did not go wrong, but I don't have to have my desires met. When they do go wrong, I can stand it, *and I can see that my life is made up of the good, the bad and the neutral.*'
Disqualifying the positive (You reject positive experiences by insisting they 'don't count' for some reason or other, thus maintaining a negative view that cannot be contradicted by your everyday experiences)	'I absolutely should not have done these foolish things and thus, *when others compliment me on the good things I have done, they are only being kind to me and forgetting these foolish things.*'
Incorporating the positive into a complex view of your experiences (You accept positive experiences and locate these into the complexity of positive, negative and neutral features of life)	'I would have preferred not to have done these foolish things, but that does not mean that I absolutely should not have done them. *When others compliment me on the good things I have done, I can accept these compliments as being genuine even though I also did some foolish things which the others may also have recognized.*'

Thinking distortion and realistic alternative	Illustration
Mind-reading (You arbitrarily conclude that someone is reacting negatively to you, and you don't bother to check this out. You regard your thought as a fact)	'I made some errors in the PowerPoint presentation that I absolutely should not have made and *when I looked at my boss, I thought he was thinking how hopeless I was, and therefore he did think this.*'
Owning and checking one's thoughts about the reactions of others (You may think someone is reacting negatively to you, but you check it out with the other person rather than regarding your thought as fact)	'I would have preferred not to have made some errors in the PowerPoint presentation, but that does not mean that I absolutely should not have made them. *I thought that my boss thought that I was hopeless, but I quickly realized that this was my thought rather than his and resolved to ask him about this in the morning.*'
Fortune-telling (You anticipate that things will turn out badly, and you feel convinced that your prediction is an already established fact)	'Because I failed at this simple task which I absolutely should not have done, *I think that I will get a very bad appraisal and thus this will happen.*'
Owning and checking one's thoughts about what will happen in the future (You anticipate that things may turn out badly, but you regard that as a prediction that needs examining against the available data, not an established fact)	'I would have preferred not to have failed at this simple task, but I do not have to be immune from doing so. *I may get a very bad appraisal, but this is unlikely since I have done far more good than bad at work during the last year.*'
'Always' and 'never' thinking (When something bad happens, you conclude that it will always happen and/or that the good alternative will never occur)	'Because my present conditions of living must be good and actually are so bad and so intolerable, *they'll always be this way and I'll never have any happiness.*'
Balanced thinking about the future (When something bad happens you recognize that while it may happen again, it is not inevitable that it will and it is very unlikely that it will always occur. Also, you recognize that the good alternative may well occur in the future and that it is very unlikely that it will never happen)	'I would like my present conditions of living to be good, but they don't have to be that way. They are bad right now and difficult to tolerate, *but it does not follow that they will always be that way, and I can be happy again.*'

Thinking distortion and realistic alternative	Illustration
Magnification (When something bad happens, you exaggerate its negativity)	'I made a faux pas when introducing my new colleague which I absolutely should not have done and it's awful that I did so. *This will have a very negative effect on my career.*'
Keeping things in realistic perspective (When something bad happens, you view it in its proper perspective)	'I wish I had not made the faux pas when introducing my new colleague, but I do not have to be exempt from saying such silly things. It's bad that I did so, but hardly the end of the world, *and while people may remember it for a day or two, I doubt that it will have much lasting impact on my career.*'
Minimization (You inappropriately shrink things until they appear tiny; these can be your own desirable qualities or other people's imperfections)	'I must do outstandingly well and I am completely useless when I do not so. *When I make mistakes, I am fully to blame for this and it has nothing to do with bad luck. And when I seemingly do well, this is the result of luck and anyone could have done this. However, when others make mistakes, there is a good reason for this or they were unlucky.*'
Using the same balanced perspective for self and others (When you do something good and/or others do something bad, you can recognize such behaviour for what it is)	'I want to do outstandingly well, but I do not have to do so. I am not useless when I do not so. Thus, when I make mistakes, I may be fully responsible or it may be down to bad luck. *And when I do well, this may be the result of luck, but it may be because I fully deserved to do well. When others make mistakes, they may have been unlucky or they may be fully responsible for their mistakes.*'

Thinking distortion and realistic alternative	Illustration
Emotional reasoning (You assume that your negative emotions necessarily reflect the way things really are: 'I feel it, therefore it must be true')	'Because I have performed so poorly, as I absolutely should not have done, I feel as if everybody will remember my poor performance and my strong feeling proves that they will.'
Sound reasoning based on thinking and feeling	'I wish that I had not performed so poorly, but that does not mean that I absolutely should not have done so. I think and feel that people will have different responses to my performance: some negative and nasty, some compassionate and empathic and some neutral, and this is probably the case.'
Personalization (When a negative event occurs involving you which you may or may not be primarily responsible for, you see yourself definitely as the cause of it)	'I am involved in a group presentation and things are not going well. Since I am acting worse than I absolutely should act and the audience is laughing, I am sure they are laughing only at me.'
Realistic attribution (When a negative event occurs involving you which you may or may not be primarily responsible for, you acknowledge that you may be the cause of it, but you don't assume that you definitely are. Rather, you view the event from the whole perspective before making an attribution of cause which is likely to be realistic)	'I am involved in a group presentation and things are not going well. I am acting worse than I would like to do, but do not demand that I must do, and the audience is laughing. I am not sure who or what they are laughing at, and indeed, some might be laughing with us and not at us.'

Having fully presented the ABCs of CBT, which should be seen as the foundations of what I will discuss in the rest of the book, let me briefly review what CBT has to offer as a method of therapeutic self-help.

What CBT has to offer

Before I get on to the heart of the book, which concerns dealing healthily with the great challenges of life so that you can move on with your life rather be bogged down, I will briefly tell you what I think CBT has to offer you.

CBT has a logical structure

I hope I have made clear while discussing CBT's ABC model that CBT offers a logical structure in understanding both your unhealthy and your healthy responses to life's challenges. It also offers a logical structure in addressing your unhealthy responses. As I have shown you, when you disturb yourself about a particular adversity, you do so primarily because you hold one or more irrational beliefs about that adversity. Then you will tend to act in certain unconstructive ways and think in ways that are grossly distorted and skewed in a negative direction. If you do act and think in these ways, you serve to unwittingly strengthen your irrational beliefs.

The logical structure of CBT encourages you to identify, examine and change these irrational beliefs to their rational alternatives and to act and think in ways that are consistent with these developing rational beliefs. If you do so, and do so consistently and repeatedly, you will strengthen your conviction in these rational beliefs and weaken your conviction in the previously and often strongly held irrational beliefs.

CBT is problem-focused

Unlike many approaches to counselling and psychotherapy, CBT focuses on your problems as you see them. CBT then helps you to assess each problem by looking at specific examples of your problem, one at a time, and by using the ABC framework so you can understand: what you are particularly disturbed about; the emotional, behavioural and thinking components of your disturbed response; and, crucially, the irrational beliefs that underpin and account for your disturbed response. If you have several disturbed responses about the same adversity, CBT advises you to deal with these problems one at a time.

In taking this problem-oriented stance, CBT encourages you to keep a present-centred and future-oriented focus with respect to your problems, and only to go back to the past if doing so will help you deal with your problems as they exist in the present or as they may become manifest in the future.

CBT is goal-directed

If CBT is problem-focused, it is also goal-directed. It encourages you to set goals with respect to each of the problems that you have identified. As far as is feasible, CBT encourages the setting of SMART goals. SMART is an acronym for:

S = Specific
M = Measurable
A = Achievable
R = Realistic
T = Time-bound

In addition, CBT encourages you to set goals at different levels. Thus, if you are disturbed about an adversity and that adversity is restricting your life, CBT would first encourage you to deal with your disturbance (disturbance-related goals) and to experience healthy negative emotions rather than unhealthy negative emotions about the adversity. Then, free from the effects of disturbance, you can set goals to address the adversity as effectively as you can.

CBT can be learned

In my view, perhaps one of the best things that CBT has to offer you in your quest to deal effectively with life's challenges is that you can learn its skills and methods and apply it for yourself, without the ongoing support of a therapist.

Of course, as a therapist myself, I would be the first to put the case for working with a therapist, but this may not always be possible for you. If this is the case then do not despair, because you *can* put into practice what you learn in this book. However, just reading will not help you. In the same way as reading a book on cooking will not help you to cook unless you get into the kitchen and put the instructions into practice, so you will have to apply what you learn. Practice may not make perfect, but it is a requirement for getting the most from CBT.

CBT encourages realistic expectations about what you can gain

The final point I want to make about what CBT has to offer you is that it encourages you to have realistic expectations about what you can achieve from the therapy. It argues that as a human you cannot elimi-nate or eradicate disturbed feelings. Rather, it helps you to see that you can learn to identify these feelings once you begin to experience them, and can then apply CBT methods of self-change to address them before you unwittingly perpetuate them with unconstructive behaviour and further distorted thinking. Keep this set of realistic expectations in mind as you read the rest of the book and as you apply what you learn there.

2

Dealing with personal limitations

Introduction

This book is devoted to common but significant life challenges that, unless we are very fortunate in life, we all face at one time or another. When I introduced the ABC model of CBT in Chapter 1, I referred to 'A' as an adversity which can be viewed as an event that occurs (or that you think has occurred) which is negative in nature and about which you disturb yourself if you hold one or more irrational beliefs about the event. However, it is also possible to regard such negative events or adversities as a challenge, because they provide you with the opportunity of responding to them in a constructive (rather than unconstructive) manner, especially if you can develop and maintain a set of rational beliefs about them. Please bear in mind as you read this book that when I refer to 'adversities' and 'challenges', I mean the same thing.

You have personal limitations

I have been writing self-help books for about 20 years now, and in doing so I try to be as realistic as possible about what people can achieve as they embark on the difficult process of personal change. Thus, I have not and will not promise you that I can make you slim, rich, popular – or anything else, come to that. I will not do so for two reasons. First, I can't make you achieve anything. Why not? Because I am not responsible for initiating and maintaining the changes that you may wish to make. I am responsible for informing you about a particular approach to personal change known as Cognitive Behavioural Therapy (CBT) and showing you how to apply CBT concepts in your own life. However, I am not responsible for whether or not you actually put these ideas into practice: you are! The second reason I do not claim to be able to change you is that I do not know whether the changes you wish to make are those of which you are capable.

Also, I have not and will not encourage you in the idea that you can achieve anything that you want to achieve. This is because you can't!

Despite what some self-help gurus might tell you, you have limitations as a human being, and if you don't identify and work within the constraints of these limitations then you are setting yourself up for a fall when you try to reach unrealistic goals.

In this chapter, then, I will help you to accept and not disturb yourself about your personal limitations. Relevant to this book, there are five types of limitations that I have in mind: those due to inherited tendencies, the constraints of your personality, intellect and temperament and your physical limitations.

Let me consider these briefly one by one.

Inherited tendencies

An inherited tendency is just that – a tendency to feel, think and act in certain unhealthy ways (for the purposes of this book) that you have inherited from your parents and their forebears. An example of such a tendency would be bipolar affective disorder (BPD), which used to be known as manic depression. This condition is characterized by extreme changes of mood, from mania to severe depression. It has been found to have a significant genetic loading, which means that in our terms it represents a tendency to mood swings that is largely inherited. I will use the example of BPD when discussing how to deal constructively with personal limitations due to such an inherited tendency. It is important to recognize that while there is nothing you can do to eradicate such a tendency, there are plenty of things you can do to manage it in order to limit its pernicious effects.

Personality constraints

People vary according to their personality characteristics and, whether these develop through nature or nurture or a combination of the two, you are likely be constrained by these characteristics. For example, let's suppose that I score highly on the personality characteristic of introversion. This means, among other things, that I am not very socially outgoing. Now, if it is my goal to become much more socially outgoing, I am likely to be limited concerning how extroverted I can become in a sustained, ongoing and natural sense. Thus, I cannot become who I want to become because I will be constrained by my natural personality. Consequently, I don't see CBT as being designed to bring about personality change. Rather, I see it as a way of helping people to be healthy within the context of their personality.

Intellectual constraints

Sadly, not everyone can be a genius! When it comes to intellectual ability, if we plot this on a graph, we find that people are distributed along a bell-shaped curve with most found, by definition, within the average intellectual range and a minority found towards the intellectually challenged and the intellectually gifted points of the curve. While it is true that there are cognitive abilities other than intellectual ones, it is sad that many people condemn themselves for their lack of achievement when in reality it is impossible for them to achieve their aspirations given their intellectual constraints.

Temperament constraints

The final set of constraints that I wish to discuss concerns those that are based on temperament. Research has shown that differences in our temperament can be discerned at a very early age. For example, some infants are highly active and others are relatively inactive, as observed by their body movements when they are born. Such differences seem to be maintained across the lifespan. Consequently, if you have a very active temperament and your goal is to be more calm and chilled, then you are probably doomed to disappointment and to disturbance if you hold a set of irrational beliefs about not achieving your goals.

Physical limitations

We all have physical limitations, although some of these are only limitations because of our demands. Severe facial disfigurement can be seen as a true significant physical limitation because it may well interfere with you finding a job and developing relationships with the opposite sex. Being a size 12 when you demand that you have to be a size 8 is a physical limitation that is more in the eye of the dress-wearer than of other people, but it is a physical limitation in your mind until you challenge your demand that you have to be a size 8 when you are a size 12.

Our personal limitations: what we disturb ourselves about and how to address these disturbances

In Chapter 1, I outlined the four irrational beliefs that underpin much psychological disturbance about life's challenges and the four alternative rational beliefs that underpin a more constructive response to these challenges.

My view is that you have a choice about whether you adopt a set of rational or irrational beliefs when faced with the fact of having a personal limitation. Please bear this fact in mind as I outline the common irrational beliefs that people hold about personal limitations and the common inferences that they make about these limitations. As I do so, I will keep the term 'personal limitation' general so you can think of your particular personal limitation as the discussion unfolds.

In the remainder of this chapter, I will detail the impact that irrational beliefs have on people's subsequent emotional, behavioural and cognitive functioning. I will then show you how you can respond healthily to these irrational beliefs, develop the alternative set of rational beliefs and think and act in ways that strengthen these rational beliefs.

Dealing with the personal limitations themselves

I will begin our discussion by considering how we disturb ourselves about the very existence of our personal limitations and how we can best address our disturbance. I will consider the major inferences that we make about these limitations and relevant disturbances in later sections.

Identify and challenge your rigid beliefs about your personal limitation and develop a flexible belief about it instead

When you have a personal limitation which yields negative consequences, it is healthy not to like this grim reality and to prefer that this was not the case. The real danger is then to transform this desire into a rigid demand by saying that, because this personal limitation has negative effects and it is unfair that you have it, therefore it must not exist. This demand might make sense if it succeeded in getting rid of this personal limitation, but unfortunately it doesn't. All it does is to add disturbance to the mix, as shown here:

Personal limitation × rigid belief = disturbance

Also, if you demand that you must not have a particular personal limitation, then you may deny that you actually have such a tendency. This process of denial may impede you from taking appropriate steps to adjust healthily to the limitation.

You might argue that you would not be disturbed if you did not have the personal limitation, and this would be true. But the reality is that you do have it, and the reason you are disturbed about this is not the existence of the personal limitation itself but your rigid belief about it. Thus, in the equation presented above, the only part that you can address if you want not to be disturbed about the personal limitation is your demand.

Addressing your demand involves still acknowledging that you would prefer not to have the personal limitation, but also realizing that it does not follow that you must not have it. Sadly, if it exists, it must be the way it is. If it could be different, you could rid yourself of your personal limitation simply by demanding that you did not have it. Unfortunately, as I have shown you, you just can't do that. So when you hold a flexible belief about your personal limitation, you don't like the fact that you have it (i.e. you are dissatisfied), but you are not disturbed about it, as shown in the following equation:

Personal limitation × flexible belief = non-disturbed dissatisfaction

Also, if you hold a flexible belief about having a particular personal limitation, then you will accept that you have the limitation rather than deny that you have it, as you would tend to do if you held a rigid demand. This flexible belief would thus aid you in the adjustment process by encouraging you to take appropriate steps to minimize the negative effects of the personal limitation.

Identify and challenge your extreme beliefs about your personal limitation and develop non-extreme beliefs instead

As I pointed out in Chapter 1, extreme beliefs tend to stem from rigid beliefs, while non-extreme beliefs tend to stem from flexible beliefs. Thus, after you have identified and challenged your rigid demand about your personal limitation and have begun to develop your flexible belief, you need to identify and challenge your extreme beliefs and start to develop their non-extreme-belief alternatives.

While it is not universally the case, it is a good rule of thumb to identify and challenge the main extreme belief that stems from your rigid belief. As discussed in Chapter 1, this will be one of the following:

- an awfulizing belief;
- a low frustration tolerance (LFT) belief; or
- a depreciation belief.

The healthy, non-extreme alternatives to these beliefs are:

- a non-awfulizing belief;
- a high frustration tolerance (HFT) belief; and
- an acceptance belief.

What to do when your main extreme belief is an awfulizing belief

When your main extreme belief about your personal limitation is an awfulizing belief, you believe that it is the end of the world that you have this limitation and that nothing can be worse. This gross extreme exaggeration will only lead you to focus on the personal limitation to the exclusion of everything else. You will thus tend to see the world through the lens of your personal limitation and you will focus on what you can't do rather than consider what you can do. Consequently, you will avoid activities that you think you can't do, won't try things that you may or may not be able to do, and end up thinking that you are much more limited than you actually are.

In responding to an awfulizing belief about your personal limitation, you need to show yourself that while having the personal limitation is bad, it is not the end of the world. This will help you keep an open mind about what you can and cannot do in life as a result of having your personal limitation, and you will test out your interpretations in this regard by trying things that you think you may or may not be able to do. You will also focus on what you can do in life as well as on what you can't do, and by actively engaging in the former you will see yourself as far less limited than you would if you held the aforementioned extreme awfulizing belief.

What to do when your main extreme belief is a low frustration tolerance (LFT) belief

When your main extreme belief about your personal limitation is an LFT belief, you believe that you cannot tolerate having this limitation. This means that you feel on the edge of disintegration and will do all you can to avoid being confronted with the limitation in case you do disintegrate. Apart from causing you to avoid all reminders of your personal limitation, this gross extreme exaggeration of your inability to tolerate having the personal limitation will lead you to see yourself as highly vulnerable and to seek security from outside yourself. As with an awfulizing belief, your LFT belief about your personal limitation will lead you to focus on what you can't do rather than on what you can do.

In responding to an LFT belief about your personal limitation, you need to show yourself that while it is a struggle putting up with having the personal limitation, it is not intolerable. Thus, you need to show yourself both that you can tolerate it and that it is worth it to you to do so. Here you will need to list and be mindful of these reasons. This will again help you keep an open mind about what you can and cannot do in life as a result of having your personal limitation, and you will see for yourself what you can and cannot do. You will not avoid reminders of your personal limitation, but will see it as providing an opportunity to be resilient rather than evidence that you are on the verge of disintegration. Seeing yourself as resilient rather than vulnerable, you will actively engage in life as much as your personal limitation will permit you.

What to do when your main extreme belief is a depreciation belief

In this section, I will consider self-depreciation; I will show you how to deal with other-depreciation and life-depreciation in other chapters. When your main extreme belief about your personal limitation is a self-depreciation belief you focus on your limitation, and then you believe that it defines you (e.g. 'I am defective because I have this personal limitation'). This belief will lead you to avoid others because you think that they share this view of you. This is known as 'projection', where you unconsciously project your attitude towards yourself into the minds of others, so that you think they view you in the same way as you view yourself. Also, because you view yourself as being defective (for example) for having the personal limitation, it is as if this attitude infects the whole of your life. You think of yourself as limited in all kinds of ways and edit out thoughts of what you can do.

In responding to a self-depreciation belief, you need to see that your personal limitation is a part of you, but that it does not and cannot define you. You need to develop a truthful view of yourself that incorporates the ideas that you are complex (rather than simple) and therefore not rateable, and that you are fallible (rather than perfectible). In seeing yourself as far more than the personal limitation that you focus on, you can see life in its full richness and not coloured by your personal limitation.

This belief will encourage you to stay connected with others rather than avoid them, since you will have a balanced view of how people think of you for having the personal limitation rather than think that they all regard you as being defective. This means that you recognize that some may think negatively of you while others will view you positively or have a mixed view of you.

Once you view yourself as a complex, fallible human being for having the personal limitation, rather than being defective as a person for having it, this attitude encourages you to think of yourself as having far more potential than you do when you consider yourself as defective. Rather than edit out thoughts of what you can do, you engage and act on such thinking.

Falling short of our ideals

The problem

As I discussed at the beginning of this chapter, we live in a society that tends to encourage us to think that we can be who we want to be. Thus, we may develop ideals which we may fall short of, because of our personal shortcomings. When this happens and we disturb ourselves about this 'fall from grace', as it were, we tend to experience the emotion of shame. As I showed in my book *Overcoming Shame* (Sheldon Press, 1997), at the heart of shame are two ideas: (1) 'This personal limitation means that I have fallen short of my ideal and I must not do so'; and (2) 'I am defective for falling short of my ideal.' The latter idea is often expressed in the statement: 'There is something wrong with me if I fall short of my ideal.'

These irrational beliefs will not only lead you to feel shame, they will affect your behaviour and subsequent thinking. Thus, you will tend to think that others will think badly of you and shun you and as a result you avoid them, thus depriving yourself of the opportunity of testing out your inferences. Indeed, your avoidance will lead you to be more convinced that others will think badly of you.

Dealing with the problem

As with all the problems discussed in this book, your primary task is to respond constructively to your irrational beliefs. Of these irrational beliefs, it is your rigid beliefs that are the breeding ground for your other irrational beliefs, your unconstructive behaviour and your subsequent distorted thinking, so you need to target for change first your rigid belief and then your extreme beliefs. In this context, you need to show yourself that while you wish to achieve your ideals, you don't have to do so and as a human being you frequently won't. If you have a personal limitation that means you will fall short of your ideals, then that is quite unfortunate but hardly the end of the world. Also, does falling short of your ideal really mean that you are a defective human being? If so, then all human beings are defective, since we all fall short of our ideals. Given this fact, it is better to accept yourself as a fallible human being rather than a defective member of the human race. If you are fallible, this means that you are prone to error and this proneness cannot be eradicated. The word 'defective' has a different meaning. It means that you should be thrown away or discarded because there is something wrong with you as a human.

Developing your rational belief depends on you acting and thinking in ways that are consistent with it. Thus, it is important for you not to avoid your friends and to remind yourself that while some people may think badly of you and shun you, they will probably be a minority and others will be more favourably disposed or neutral towards you. By not avoiding other people, you will be able to judge the true reactions of others.

Frustration

The problem

When you have a personal limitation this may be a source of frustration for you, particularly if the limitation stops you from achieving a valued goal. If you disturb yourself about this frustration, you again do so because you hold two irrational beliefs: (1) 'I must not be frustrated by being unable to reach my goal because of the existence of my personal limitation'; and (2) 'I can't stand the frustration of not being able to reach my goal because of the existence of my personal limitation.' Holding these irrational beliefs, you will tend not to try and reach your goal, and will then think that, since you won't achieve this goal, you won't achieve other goals.

Dealing with the problem

When you have a personal limitation, it often follows that you will be frustrated when that limitation blocks you from achieving an important goal. Demanding that you must not be frustrated in this regard will not result in the removal of this frustration. Rather, it will increase your frustration, since this demand will lead to disturbance about your frustration. If you are truthful, you will acknowledge that while you would prefer not to be frustrated, this does not mean that you must not be, and if you are, you are!

As for the idea that you can't stand the frustration of not being able to reach your goal because of the existence of your personal limitation, this is obviously not true. You can tolerate it, although it's a struggle for you to do so. If we said to you that you could be spared the frustration in exchange for the life of a loved one, would you sacrifice that life because you couldn't tolerate being frustrated? Of course not! You can tolerate the frustration. The real questions are:

- Is it worth it to you to tolerate this frustration? Put another way, will tolerating the frustration help you to move on and deal with life productively despite the existence of your personal limitation? If you really think about it, you will see that the answer to these questions is 'yes'.
- Are you prepared to tolerate the frustration and move on? Tolerating frustration is a choice. You could do so, or you could practise your LFT belief and, in addition, feel sorry for yourself that not only do you have the personal limitation but you experience the frustration that the limitation brings you in life. If you want to move on, practise your HFT belief, but if you want to feel miserable and be disturbed, practise your LFT belief.

If you hold the rational beliefs detailed above, even if you can't reach your initial goal you will think that there are other goals you can achieve. Behaviourally, your rational beliefs will encourage you to persist in striving to achieve your original goal and to try to find a way around your personal limitation. If you can't find one, you will change your goal.

Unfairness

The problem

When you compare yourself to your peer group it may be that you are the only one in the group with your particular personal limitation. When you disturb yourself about the seeming unfairness of having the limitation when others you know do not have it, you believe the following: 'It is unfair that I have this personal limitation when others that I know don't. Life must not be so unfair to me and it's terrible that it is. Poor me!' Consequently, you will feel self-pity. This irrational belief may well lead you to act in an unconstructive way by withdrawing from your friends, and if you do so you further deprive yourself of pleasure. This may then lead to a further bout of feeling sorry for yourself. When you are in a self-pity frame of mind – brought about, don't forget, by your irrational beliefs about the presumed unfairness – you will tend to think of other ways in which you are disadvantaged in life and to edit out areas in life where you are, in fact, fortunate.

Dealing with the problem

It is important that you realize that while the fairness of being free of your personal limitation would be nice, it does not have to exist in your case. If it is unfair that you have the personal limitation, that is unfortunately the way it is. Demanding fairness does not get rid of unfairness; it just gives you the additional unfairness of disturbance. Also, it is rough that such unfairness exists but it is hardly the end of the world, and while it is true that when you have a personal limitation you are in a poor situation, it does not follow that you are a poor person who has to pity yourself. You are a non-poor person who is in a poor situation.

This rational belief will encourage you to stay involved with your friends rather than withdraw from them, thus not experiencing the additional unfairness of depriving yourself of pleasure. This rational belief will also help you to have a balanced view of the fairnesses and unfairnesses of your life.

I will look at how to deal with unfairness more generally in Chapter 8.

Being different

The problem

In the previous section, I discussed the situation where you have a personal limitation, mix with people who do not share that limitation and focus on the seeming unfairness of this situation. In this section, I will deal with the same objective situation, but where you focus on the difference between yourself and these other people. When you focus on the difference between yourself and others and disturb yourself about this, you are probably holding a number of irrational beliefs. First, you are rigidly demanding that you must not be different from the others and because you are this leads you to exaggerate the differences and minimize the similarities between you and the others. Second, you transform the non-extreme idea that it is bad to be different from others with respect to your personal limitation to the extreme idea that it is horrible to be different. This awfulizing belief tends to lead to the sense that you are isolated from others and will lead you to see yourself as being lonely in the future. Third, you will tend to over-generalize from the idea that you are different from your comparison group with respect to your personal limitation to the idea that you are different from them, full stop. When you see your 'self' as different and you are disturbed about this, this sense of being different as a person tends to be accompanied by other self-depreciating ideas about yourself (e.g. 'I am a freak', 'I am unlovable' and 'I am disgusting').

The three irrational beliefs that I have just discussed not only have an impact on your subsequent thinking, as outlined above, they also have a profound impact on your behaviour. Thus, these three beliefs will tend to lead you either to hide or to cover up your personal limitation so that others do not see it, or to isolate yourself from others. When you remain with others and try to hide your personal limitation from them, your underlying irrational beliefs will render you (1) anxious about the possibility that you will be discovered; (2) depressed about your need to hide from others; and (3) alienated from them psychologically, even though you are in their physical presence and interacting with them. You will tend to feel an impostor when you are with them, but see no way out of this.

When you isolate yourself from others, you will then tend to focus on your isolation and tend to disturb yourself about this. This will increase your isolation and you will trap yourself in a vicious circle of ever increasing disturbance and isolation.

Dealing with the problem

As before, you need to address your irrational beliefs effectively and develop a set of rational beliefs that will lead you to think clearly about being different and to act constructively in this area of your life.

The first step in this process is for you to develop and act on a flexible belief about being different with respect to having a personal limitation that others don't have. You do this by being honest and recognizing that you would prefer to be the same as your peers who do not share your personal limitation. However, you also appreciate that you don't have to have your preference met, and that if you are different from them in this respect then that is the way it unfortunately is and has to be. Why does it have to be that way? Because, sadly, all the factors are in place for you to be different from them, in the sense that you have the personal limitation and they don't.

The second step is for you to take the horror out of being different from your reference group without taking the badness out of this state of affairs. Regarding such difference as being horrible means that nothing could be worse than this. A moment's reflection indicates that this is not the case. As Smokey Robinson's mother told him: 'Son, from the day you are born till you ride in the hearse, there is nothing so bad that it couldn't be worse.' So, keep things in proportion. By all means assert that it is bad being different from your peers, but convince yourself that such difference is neither horrible, terrible nor the end of the world.

Finally, while it is important that you acknowledge that you are different from your reference group in that you have a particular personal limitation and they don't, it is even more important that you counter the idea that this proves you are a different person from them. Being different in one respect is light years away from being different as a whole person. Also, you need to respond effectively to the idea that you are a freak, unlovable or a disgusting person. You are none of these things. Even if your personal limitation is freakish, difficult to love or disgusting, this hardly makes you a freak, unlovable or disgusting, since your personal limitation is only a small aspect of you. It does not define you unless you believe that it does.

If you hold these three rational beliefs, you will view your personal limitation and others' reactions to it in a realistic context, and you will stay connected with others without fear that you may be discovered for having a personal limitation and without putting on a façade. Your rational beliefs help you to disclose the fact of your personal limitation when it is realistically safe and advantageous to you to do so.

Mildred

Mildred is a 38-year-old woman who, in her late teens, was diagnosed with bipolar affective disorder, a psychiatric condition that she inherited from her mother's side of the family. Mildred found it difficult to accept the fact that she had BPD and periodically came off her medication, with disastrous consequences. However, her CBT therapist encouraged her to accept herself for having the condition, and this helped her to remain on her medication, with constructive results.

What were the ingredients of Mildred's therapy that you can learn from if you have an inherited tendency which may impact negatively on your life?

Adopting a flexible attitude towards the inherited tendency

Mildred's therapist helped her to see that she was disturbing herself about her bipolar affective disorder by demanding that she should not have it. Mildred was urged to accept that, while she would much prefer not to have this inherited condition, this did not mean that she must not have it, no matter how unfair it was that she did have it. This helped her to accept, but actively dislike, the fact that she had bipolar affective disorder and to take and commit to remain on her medication.

Taking the horror out of the inherited tendency

Another part of Mildred's disturbance was due to the fact that she focused on the bad aspects of having bipolar affective disorder and then turned these into end-of-the-world horrors. When she did this, she felt hopeless and helpless: hopeless in that all seemed black in the future, and helpless because she considered that there was nothing she could do to help herself.

Her therapist agreed with Mildred that having bipolar affective disorder was handicapping in a number of respects and that this was a bad state of affairs. However, he helped her to discriminate between the idea that it is bad to be handicapped and the belief that this is the end of the world. As Mildred came to accept and implement this distinction, she saw that there was a lot she could do to help herself. Thus, she could take her medication rigorously, develop a healthy sleeping regimen, drink alcohol in moderation and seek support from friends when she was feeling particularly vulnerable. Seeing that she could do all this to help herself gave Mildred hope for the future, in that there was a lot she could gain from life if she chose to help herself.

Developing self-acceptance

Before seeking therapeutic help, Mildred regarded herself as being defective for having bipolar affective disorder. She realized that this was an inherited condition, but regarded herself as being tainted for having this condition. This led her to hide this grim reality, at times from herself and most of the time from others. To prove to herself that she was not defective, she engaged in pursuits that rendered her vulnerable. Thus, she would drink too much alcohol and go shopping with her rich friends, getting caught up with the excitement of these shopping expeditions and spending too much into the bargain.

Mildred's therapist helped her to identify her self-depreciation belief and to see the effects that she experienced in holding the belief. He helped Mildred to see the difference between having a handicap and being defective, and that the latter did not follow on from the former. Mildred came to appreciate deeply that being human involves living with a complex mixture of abilities, lack of abilities and handicaps, and that while having bipolar affective disorder was handicapping in a number of respects, this did not mean that she was defective as a human being. The more Mildred accepted herself as a complex, fallible, unrateable, human being rather than as being defective, the more she began to admit to herself and to others that she had bipolar affective disorder. This helped her to take healthy steps to deal effectively with her personal limitation.

In the next chapter, I will consider how you can best deal with and move on from the losses in your life.

3

Dealing with loss

Introduction

Aaron Beck, the founder of Cognitive Therapy, a specific and popular approach within CBT, introduced the concept of the personal domain in the mid-1970s. The personal domain represents the people, other beings, objects and ideas that we hold dear. This chapter is focused on loss and, more specifically, the losses that we actually experience or think we have experienced from our personal domain.

As such, according to the ABCs of CBT, loss comes under 'A'.

Loss can be experienced as an adversity or as an opportunity. In this chapter, I will begin by regarding it as an adversity, but will show what you need to do to transform it into an opportunity.

Elements of loss

If you have experienced a significant loss, the following elements comprise that loss:

1 a person (or other being), an object or concept that you prize;
2 the person (or other being), object or concept occupying or having occupied an important place in your personal domain;
3 a sense that you no longer have that person (or being), object or concept in your life as you once did.

Loss implies change, and a change that you consider to be for the worse, especially at the time of the loss and until you have engaged in a process known as mourning. This process enables you to grieve your loss and move on. However, even after you have successfully engaged in the mourning process you may still see the loss as a negative change, although if you have properly grieved your loss you may see that it has positive aspects as well.

Common losses

The National Association for Loss and Grief in Victoria, Australia, lists a number of common losses on its website (<www.nalagvic.org.au>). These include:

- death;
- separation, divorce, relationship breakdown;
- loss of family unit, children leaving home;
- adoption or relinquishment of children;
- unemployment, retirement;
- loss of role, status;
- loss of health, amputation, removal of an organ;
- loss of homeland, culture, language;
- loss of a pet;
- loss of possessions, burglary, car theft;
- loss of freedom;
- disability;
- loss of youth, body image;
- infertility, stillbirth, miscarriage, abortion;
- missing person;
- loss of dreams, hopes, expectations;
- caring for someone with a chronic or life-threatening disease;
- moving house, state, country.

In this chapter, I will focus both on the losses themselves and on the adversities that are linked to loss, and show you how to deal with these realistically and constructively so that you can move on with your life. In doing so, I will particularly concentrate on those beliefs that lead you to get stuck in the grieving or mourning process and will show you how to develop alternatives to these beliefs, alternatives that will aid the moving-on process.

Losses: what we disturb ourselves about, and how to address these disturbances

In Chapter 1, I outlined the four irrational beliefs that underpin much psychological disturbance about life's adversities and challenges, and the four alternative rational beliefs that underpin a more constructive response to these situations. You might find it useful to review that material before proceeding with the rest of this chapter.

Dealing with the loss itself

In this part of the chapter, I will discuss how to deal with losses themselves and not with issues related to the losses. I will deal with this
latter issue in the next section.

Identify and challenge your rigid beliefs about your loss and develop a flexible belief about it instead

When you experience a loss, it is healthy to prefer that it did not
happen and to regard the loss as a very negative state of affairs. Again,
the problem occurs when you transform this desire into a rigid demand
by saying that because this loss is unwanted, it absolutely should not
have occurred. This demand does not rewind reality to the point where
the loss had not occurred. It would be sensible if it did! Rather, it only
succeeds in creating disturbance about the loss, as shown below.

Loss × rigid belief = disturbance

Also, if you demand that the loss absolutely should not have occurred,
then you may deny that it has occurred. Now, the presence of denial
is not necessarily unhealthy if it is a temporary phenomenon. Indeed,
some grief theorists argue that it is a natural response to experiencing
a loss. However, when you get stuck in denial then this is evidence
that you are thinking rigidly, and this thinking therefore needs to be
addressed.

Responding to your rigid belief about loss involves acknowledging
that you would prefer not to have experienced the loss, but also realizing that it does not follow that you must not have done so. Sadly,
loss is a part of your life and everyone's life, and often factors outside
your control dictate when a loss in your life occurs. Thus, if a loved one
dies then he or she died because of factors that very often have little
or nothing to do with you. Sadly and regrettably, if that is reality then
that is the way it has to be. Reality must be reality!

So when you hold a flexible belief about loss, you actively dislike it
and effectively grieve the loss, but you are not disturbed about it, as
shown in the following equation:

Loss × flexible belief = non-disturbed grief

Also, if you hold a flexible belief about experiencing a loss, meaning
that you would prefer, but do not insist, that the loss absolutely should
not have happened, then you will be more likely to accept that the
loss has happened than to deny it, as you would tend to do if you held
a rigid demand about the loss. This flexible belief will aid you in the

mourning process by encouraging you to fully acknowledge your loss and grieve appropriately.

Identify and challenge your extreme beliefs about your loss and develop non-extreme beliefs instead

If you recall, extreme beliefs tend to stem from rigid beliefs, while non-extreme beliefs tend to stem from flexible beliefs. Thus, after you have identified and challenged your rigid demand about your loss and have begun to develop your flexible belief, you need to identify and challenge your extreme beliefs about the loss and start to develop their non-extreme-belief alternatives.

As I discussed earlier in the book, it is best to identify and challenge the main extreme belief that stems from your rigid belief. This will be:

- an awfulizing belief;
- an LFT belief; or
- a depreciation belief.

The healthy, non-extreme alternatives to these beliefs are:

- a non-awfulizing belief;
- an HFT belief; and
- an acceptance belief.

What to do when your main extreme belief is an awfulizing belief

When your main extreme belief about your loss is an awfulizing belief, you believe that it is the end of the world that you have experienced the loss and that nothing good can possibly happen again. If you hold this belief temporarily, then this may well be a normal part of grief. However, if you get bogged down in the belief in an enduring way then you need to respond to this extreme exaggeration, as either it will lead you to focus on the loss to the exclusion of everything else or you will attempt to banish all thoughts and reminders of the loss from your mind. Either way, your awfulizing belief serves to prevent you from mourning your loss, so that you will not be able to move on.

In responding to an awfulizing belief about your loss, you need to acknowledge that while losing something important to you is bad, it changes your world but does not represent the end of your world. It may feel like the end, but this is an example of emotional reasoning, where you use your feelings as evidence of the truth of your awfulizing belief rather than what they are, the consequences of holding this belief.

One reason people are reluctant to surrender their awfulizing belief

is that its alternative does not seem to do proper justice to the serious-
ness of the loss. Such people argue that it is bad if you lose a cheap
pen, but if you lose a job surely that really is terrible. CBT has a good
response to this criticism. When you say that it is bad, but not terrible, to lose something important to you, the extent of the badness
matches the strength of the loss. Thus, if your loss is slight then your
evaluation of badness will match this. Similarly, if your loss is great
then your evaluation of the badness of this loss will also match this.
The important thing to remember here is that, no matter how bad the
loss is when it happens, it is rarely if ever the end of the world, even if
it feels as though it is.

The relative evaluation of badness, which is the heart of the non-
extreme non-awfulizing belief, enables you to face up to your loss and
process it in a way that reflects the badness of the loss on the one hand
and the lack of horror on the other. This will help you to integrate the
loss into your life and encourage you to move on, without minimizing
the importance of the loss.

What to do when your main extreme belief is an LFT belief

When your main extreme belief about your loss is an LFT belief, you
believe that you cannot survive in the face of this loss. While this is
an understandable way to think when you have just experienced this
loss, it is usually a time-limited way of thinking and you will generally
think differently after you have processed the loss. However, if your
thoughts do not shift away from this idea, you will need to stand back
and re-evaluate it.

In responding to an LFT belief about your loss, you need to show
yourself that while it is a struggle surviving the loss, you can do so.
Indeed, even when you think that you won't survive, you are in fact
surviving, and even though you may think that you have forfeited your
capacity to live and be happy again, you haven't.

You may experience an obstacle about giving up your LFT and developing an alternative HFT belief. Thus, if you have lost a person who has
been central to your life, you may think that you are betraying him or
her by thinking that you can survive and be happy. If so, think carefully about this. If you had died and your loved one lived on, would
you like that person to think that it was impossible to live without you?
It may sound romantic, but wishing that a loved one will be forever
miserable after your death does not sound like love to me. Does it to
you? Probably not. So, it is very likely that your loved one would want
you to move on with your life too. Honour his or her memory by
doing so. Moving on after a loss does not mean that you will not think

about what or who you have lost. Far from it. It means that you are engaging with life again, but will still think about your loss. The more you engage with life, the less frequent and less painful your thoughts will be. But you will, in all probably, never forget what or who you have lost.

What to do when your main extreme belief is a self-depreciation belief

When your main extreme belief about your loss is a self-depreciation belief, you think that your loss defines you. I will discuss worthless-ness beliefs about loss later in the chapter, when I consider loss-related adversities. For the moment, let me make this point. When you lose something or someone and you just focus on that loss, if you depreciate yourself you tend to think that you are nothing without the object or person that you have lost. This belief will lead you to withdraw from life because your 'I am nothing' belief will lead you to think that there is no point to your life any more. Again, if you hold this belief tempor-arily this is probably an understandable part of the mourning process, but if this idea becomes fixed and endures over time then you need to address it, because it has clear unhealthy effects.

In responding to a self-depreciation 'I am nothing' belief, you need to see that you have equated your whole self with the object or person that you have lost. The reality is that you are still someone, even though you have lost something or someone of great importance to you. My late colleague Howard Young from West Virginia would have argued that you are not less of a person for your loss. Rather, you are a person with less. In this attitude, you are constant. You don't change, but what you *have* changes. Difficult as it may be to acknowledge, you are still someone, whether or not you have or don't have the prized object or prized person in your life.

As I pointed out to you in a previous chapter, you need to develop a complex view of yourself, so that while you can acknowledge the pain of your loss, you can also retain the idea that you are intact in the face of this loss and are certainly not 'nothing'. This healthy belief will encourage you to stay engaged with life and thus protect you from a sense of hopelessness that your 'I am nothing' induces.

Having discussed how to deal effectively with the loss itself, let me now consider the main inferences that we make about losses and how not to disturb ourselves about such inferences.

Dealing with loss when you think it means rejection

The problem

When people lose a relationship, they often think that they have been rejected even when this is not the case. Some people even think that they have been rejected when their loved one has died. In keeping with the position taken in this chapter, such an inference is a typical feature of grief, where people think in many different disturbed and irrational ways. The problem is not that they think this way. The problem occurs when they get stuck in this mode of thinking and can't move on with their lives. So in this section I am going to assume (1) that you have lost a person; (2) that you think this means that you have been rejected; and (3) that you have disturbed yourself about such rejection.

In Rational Emotive Behaviour Therapy (REBT), the approach to CBT that I am taking in this book, we recommend that when you infer rejection and you are disturbed about being rejected, you assume temporarily that you are correct in your inference. The reason we suggest this approach is that when you are disturbed you are not in an objective frame of mind to stand back and question your inference. So we suggest that you deal with your disturbed feelings first, and then question whether or not your loss means that you have been rejected.

When you disturb yourself about being rejected, you demand that this must not happen to you. In other words, your belief about being rejected is rigid. The extreme beliefs that are derived from this rigid belief tend to be either self-depreciation (e.g. 'This rejection proves that I am worthless'), LFT (e.g. 'I cannot bear the state of rejection' or, when the person feels hurt about being rejected, 'I can't stand the pain of feeling hurt') or both.

If you hold a demand and a self-depreciation belief about being rejected, your behaviour is marked by withdrawal and avoidance. Thus, you may tend to withdraw into yourself and avoid others. If you think you have been rejected romantically, you may withdraw from the dating scene and refuse to do things and go to places where you may meet someone. Holding these beliefs will also lead to distorted thinking. Thus, you may well think that as you are worthless or unlovable as a result of being rejected, then nobody will be interested in you in the future. This mode of thinking will reinforce your behavioural withdrawal and avoidance.

When your rigid belief about rejection is accompanied by LFT beliefs, then you will be motivated to avoid all memories of being rejected and to escape the intolerable feelings that stem from your irrational beliefs.

This reinforces your idea that if you don't avoid and escape the memories and/or feelings, then you will disintegrate psychologically.

Dealing with the problem

In dealing with your disturbed feelings about loss-related rejection, the most important strategy you can take is to question your rigid belief, and to develop a belief that is flexible and can help you to move on in the face of rejection. You need to show yourself that as much as you would like to be, sadly you are not immune from rejection and nor do you have to be so immune. You may have been vaccinated against a variety of illnesses when you were a child, but you weren't vaccinated against rejection. Such a vaccine has not been developed and I doubt very much whether it will ever be!

If your disturbance is centred on the idea that rejection means that you are worthless, it is important that you question this. You need to show yourself that while loss through rejection is serious, it does not and cannot define you as a person. If you thought you were worthwhile before being rejected and worthless afterwards, you are saying that this event can radically transform you. If you think about it, you will see that this is false and illogical as well as being counterproductive. You need to remind yourself that you are a complex, fallible, unrateable human being who is affected, but not fundamentally changed in terms of your worth, by the rejection. If you keep this in mind you will see that you will be loved again and you will not avoid others or withdraw into yourself.

If your disturbance about your loss-based rejection relates more to your extreme LFT belief, then after questioning your rigid belief you need to question this belief. Show yourself that while focusing on your memories of your loved one, who you have lost by rejection, is painful, it is not unbearable, and it is helpful to do so because it will help you to process your loss-based rejection, integrate it into your overall view of life where such things do happen, and move on.

The same principle also holds when dealing with your LFT belief about your hurt feelings. Such feelings are painful, but they are certainly not unbearable, and tolerating them will help you to identify, challenge and change the irrational beliefs that underpin your feelings of hurt. If you escape from such feelings you will not be motivated to make such belief change and will thus perpetuate your disturbance.

Being flexible about loss-based rejection, accepting yourself in the face of it and tolerating the memories and feelings associated with loss will help you to process the loss, think objectively about it and stay engaged with the social world. It will also help you to stand back and reconsider the idea that the loss is evidence for rejection.

Dealing with loss that you think you have deserved

When you have lost something or someone important to you, you may well think that it is unfair that you have experienced this loss. I have shown you how to deal with your disturbed feelings about unfairness in the previous chapter, and I will consider this issue in even greater detail in Chapter 8. However, you may infer that you deserved to experience this loss and disturb yourself accordingly, and it is this disturbance that I will consider in this section of the chapter.

The problem

When you think that you deserve to experience a loss, you are saying that events like losses are experienced according to whether you deserve them or not. So if you experience a loss, then you deserve to experience it. Here, the loss is considered to be some kind of punishment for some previous wrongdoing. Since it is always possible to find something wrong that you have done in the past, it is easy, if you adhere to this principle of deservingness, to think that the loss is punishment for this wrongdoing.

The real problem here is guilt and the thinking that underpins this emotion. You experience guilt (as opposed to remorse) when:

1 you think you have done the wrong thing, failed to do the right thing or hurt the feelings of someone important to you;
2 you hold a rigid belief about one or more of the above and you think that you are a bad person for doing so;
3 you think that as a bad person you deserve to be punished, and when you lose something or someone important to you, you conclude that this loss is a punishment for what you did or failed to do, or for hurting someone. This loss may be directly relevant to this event (e.g. you lose a person you have wronged) or there may be no connection between the two (e.g. you hurt your mother's feelings and then you lose your job).

From this analysis, the idea that you deserve to lose what you lost is a thinking consequence of your irrational belief about the sin of commission, the sin of omission or hurting someone.

Dealing with the problem

The best way of dealing with the 'I deserved this loss' idea is to challenge the irrational beliefs that underpin your guilt. Show yourself that if you did break your moral code, failed to live up to it or hurt someone's feelings then that was a bad thing to do, but even so there is sadly no reason why you absolutely must not break your moral code. This is not letting yourself off the hook, for you do need to take responsibility for what you did (or failed to do). However, there is no need to condemn yourself, since you are not a bad person for what you did or failed to do. Rather, you are a fallible person who did the wrong thing.

If you accept rather than condemn yourself, this will weaken the idea that experiencing a loss means that you deserved to do so. You will begin to see that losses happen for a number of reasons and are not inevitably connected to your prior bad behaviour.

Dealing with loss-related hardship

The problem

There are a number of losses that we experience that bring with them hardship of one type or another. Let's take the loss of a job. Not only have you lost something that you may have enjoyed and that helped to give you a sense of meaning, but you also have to deal with the loss of your wage or salary and the hardship that you and your family will no doubt experience.

When you disturb yourself about such hardship, you again hold a rigid belief, usually accompanied by a derived awfulizing belief or LFT belief about this hardship (e.g. 'I must not experience hardship and it is terrible that I have' or 'I must not experience hardship and I can't bear doing so'). When you hold these irrational beliefs, you tend to think that the hardship will be endless and you underestimate your ability to get yourself out of the situation. Correspondingly, you will tend to give up in your quest to redress this situation.

Also, when you take responsibility for bringing about the hardship and you disturb yourself about doing so, you tend to hold a demand accompanied by a self-depreciation belief (e.g. 'I absolutely should have discharged my responsibility better so that my family and I would not experience hardship, and I am a bad person for failing to do what I absolutely should have done'). This irrational belief may lead you to exaggerate the length of time you and your family will be exposed to such hardship and may tend to lead you not to make concerted efforts to address this situation.

Dealing with the problem

In dealing with disturbed feelings about loss-related hardship, it is important to show yourself that while it is highly undesirable to experience such hardship, it does not follow that you and those close to you must not experience it. It is important that you develop a philosophy of life that incorporates the fact that you may experience situations that you would very much prefer not to experience, and that there is no reason why you have to be exempt from doing so.

If you think that it is awful to experience such hardship, think again. No doubt it is disadvantageous to do so, but are you really saying that nothing could be worse? Think about it for a minute, and you will see that this is not the case. Many things can be worse. Let me demonstrate this quickly. If you have children, would you allow one of their limbs to be amputated if it meant that you would be spared such hardship? In all probability you would not. Why? Because you would say that having your child lose a limb would be much worse than the hardship that you are experiencing as a result of the loss. Also, good things can come from bad things. Thus, many people say that they discover the true meaning of the love and support of their family and friends when such hardship befalls them.

If you think that it is intolerable to experience such hardship, again it is important to question this belief. Let me tell you the 'Wise Rabbi' story, which helps to explain that you can tolerate what you think you can't! Many years ago in Eastern Europe a couple consulted their local rabbi, who was in those days considered to be the fount of all wisdom. The couple had recently had a child who would not stop crying, and they believed that they could not tolerate the noise and lack of sleep that ensued. Listening carefully to their concerns, the rabbi advised them to go back to their small, cramped one-bedroom dwelling and invite both sets of parents to stay. The rabbi was not to be questioned, so they did as they were told. When they came back after a month, at the rabbi's request, they were in a much worse state. Pandemonium had ensued, with both sets of parents arguing with one another, and this had the effect of increasing the loudness and frequency of their baby's crying. Hearing their heartfelt complaints, the rabbi told them to go home and bring their farmyard animals into their living quarters, and to return again in a month's time. This they did, literally on their hands and knees, for the cacophony of noise and conflict had increased markedly since their previous visit. On the verge of collapse, the couple begged the rabbi for help. The rabbi told them to go home, dispatch both sets of parents, put the animals back in the farmyard and return in a month. When they came back, the rabbi asked for an update. The parents, now smiling and relaxed, stated that the baby was as fractious as on their first visit, but in comparison to what they had been through in the previous two months, this was much easier to put up with. The moral of this story is that you can tolerate far more than you think you can. So, can you tolerate loss-related hardship? As Bob the Builder might say: 'Yes you can!'

When you take responsibility for bringing about the hardship that was induced by loss, challenge your demand and self-depreciation belief. I have showed you how to do the former, so let me concentrate on the latter.

Show yourself that you are not a bad person for failing to prevent this hardship from occurring. Convince yourself that you are a fallible human being who cannot always prevent bad things from happening. Accepting yourself in this way will help you to see that the length of time you and your family will be exposed to such hardship is likely to be finite and will lead you to make concerted efforts to address this situation.

Terence

Terence is a 41-year-old man who was made redundant from his job as managing director in an engineering firm. He disturbed himself about his loss-related hardship and the loss of meaning that he experienced, since he valued his job greatly. He did this by holding a demand and an LFT belief. His view was that he must not experience both the hardship and loss of meaning together, and that to do so was unbearable.

He helped himself by showing himself that while he was experiencing two adversities as a result of the loss, this was difficult to put up with but he could do so and it was worth it for him to do so. It would be preferable to deal with such adversities one at a time, but that did not have to be run according to his preferences.

In taking this stance about the conjoint occurrence of hardship and loss of meaning, Terence overcame his tendency to withdraw into a shell and forced himself to apply for a range of jobs, even though he was over-qualified for some of them. He soon got one such job, but refrained from attaching his self-worth to the fact that he accepted a low-status position. What mattered, he argued, was earning some money so he could help to pay the household bills.

When it came to dealing with the loss of meaning associated with leaving his job, Terence helped himself to see that he did not have to put all his meaning eggs in the managing director's basket. While such meaning was important to him, he did not have to have it and he could gain meaning in his life from a myriad of other things, such as his family, helping others less fortunate than himself and writing a book about his experiences, designed to help others cope with a similar loss.

Engaging in such activities helped Terence counteract the hopelessness that he experienced derived from his irrational beliefs. In doing so, he was able to move on from his loss and expand his view of what was important and meaningful in his life.

4

Dealing with uncertainty

Introduction

It is a truism to say that we live in an uncertain world. However, acknowledging this will not by itself help you if you have a psychological problem where uncertainty is a major feature. This is because you are not disturbed by uncertainty. Rather, you disturb yourself about uncertainty by the irrational beliefs that you hold about this state of affairs.

Now, strictly speaking we do not just disturb ourselves about uncertainty itself: we disturb ourselves when we link uncertainty with another threat to our well-being. As such, I will not deal with how we disturb ourselves about uncertainty on its own because we rarely do so. Rather, I will consider how we disturb ourselves when uncertainty is linked to some other threat.

Uncertainty: what we disturb ourselves about and how to address these disturbances

Uncertainty plays a key role in a number of anxiety-based disorders. For example, it is a key feature of worry, so-called 'fear of flying', obsessive–compulsive disorder (OCD) and health anxiety. I will briefly show the role that uncertainty plays in the first three of these problems before concentrating on health anxiety, since this is a common concern and specific enough for me to tease out the important ingredients of an uncertainty-related problem and thence show you how to respond effectively to these ingredients.

Worry

When we worry, we think we are facing an uncertainty-related threat about which we hold a set of irrational beliefs. These beliefs then lead us (1) to feel anxious or worried; (2) to produce highly distorted thinking which we consider reflects imminent reality; and (3) to act in ways that are designed to keep us safe, but which in the longer term maintain the irrational beliefs underpinning our worry.

People can worry about a great number of things, and thus to do justice to this subject would require an entire book. Suffice it to say, however, that we only worry when there is a threat to our physical, material or psychological well-being or the well-being of those that are close to us, and where there is a degree of uncertainty related to the threat.

Fear of flying

I dislike the term 'fear of flying' because it is clear that the one thing you are not afraid of is that the plane you are or will be travelling in will fly! You may think that the plane will crash or that you will lose control of yourself in some way through feelings of anxiety, but you are not worried that the plane will fly. When you think that the plane will crash, you think this way because you hold a set of irrational beliefs about the uncertainty concerning the safety of the plane you are travelling in or about to travel in. If you can't get certainty that it will land safely (and who can give you such a guarantee?) then your irrational beliefs lead you to think that it may well crash, and you interpret every unusual noise or bit of turbulence as evidence that there is imminent danger to the plane. This is why statistics are useless in the treatment of fear of flying, for they do not address the person's irrational beliefs and they remind the traveller that flying is not completely safe.

As I mentioned earlier, not having a sense of being in control is also a feature of fear of flying, and I will discuss the general issue of loss of control and how to deal with it in the next chapter.

Obsessive–compulsive disorder (OCD)

OCD is a serious condition. If you suffer from this you do need to seek professional help, and the best place to start is with your GP. However, I will briefly discuss OCD here in order to show the role that uncertainty plays in its development and maintenance. Uncertainty is not the only theme in OCD, but it is a major one. Indeed, the French used to call OCD the 'doubters' disease', which clearly indicates the role of uncertainty and doubt.

Let's take the case of Freda, who has OCD that is checking-related. For example, it takes her 45 minutes to walk away from her car once she has parked it. What happens is this. She locks the car, walks away and becomes anxious that she may not have locked it, so she goes back to check. Checking involves her putting the key in the lock and turning it. When she does this, she invariably finds that she did lock the car in the first place. However, in discovering this she has to unlock the door and then lock it again, which puts her right back to square one: in a state of uncertainty about whether or not she has locked the car.

To try to reassure herself that she has locked the door, Freda engages in a variety of behaviours which actually make her problem worse in the long run. Thus, she says out loud, 'I have locked the car,' or she writes this statement down and then reads it back to herself. Or she gets a passer-by to confirm that she has locked the car, or even gets the person to lock it for her. All of these manoeuvres can be problematic for Freda, even in the shorter term. Some of the time they reassure her, but at other times they don't. Thus, when she says out loud, 'I have locked the car,' or reads this, having written it down, she doubts whether she is doing so to reassure herself or whether the door really is locked. When the passer-by reassures her, she wonders if the person is only doing this to humour her and considers her to be weird. And if the passer-by locks the door for her, she is also in a state of doubt concerning whether or not the person has actually done so.

Even when these manoeuvres do work, in the sense that Freda feels reassured and can walk away from the car, they serve to perpetuate her problem, in that they reinforce the following irrational belief that Freda holds: 'I must know or feel sure that I have locked the car and it's terrible to be in a state of doubt.' This belief leads Freda to think that her car is bound to be stolen if she is not sure that the doors are locked. In this way, Freda has trained herself that a state of uncertainty is dangerous in that it leads to a dire consequence (i.e. her car being stolen). Consequently, she thinks that she has to rid herself of uncertainty and doubt before walking away from the car.

What Freda needs to do is to challenge her rigid idea about certainty concerning her car being locked and then train herself to walk away from the car while being in a state of uncertainty. She thus needs to acknowledge to herself and to act on this acknowledgement that feeling sure that the car is locked is a desirable state to be in, but not a necessary one. If she consistently acts on this new more rational idea and does not seek reassurance, then she will learn to walk away from the car despite what is in her mind (e.g. that the car will be stolen). She will learn that such thoughts are a manifestation of her problem and not a reliable guide to what will happen.

Health anxiety

In this section, I will deal more comprehensively with the issue of health anxiety. Health anxiety is the modern name for a condition that used to be called hypochondria. Like 'fear of flying' it is actually a misnomer, for one thing that you are decidedly not anxious about is that you are in a good state of health! Indeed, you are anxious about precisely the opposite: that you are in a state of ill health. However, since psychologists call this problem 'health anxiety', I will follow convention and do the same.

The problem

Let me begin by considering the factors in health anxiety and the role that uncertainty plays in it.

1 You identify a symptom or sign related to the possibility of ill health. This sign or symptom is ambiguous. Thus, you are in a state of uncertainty with respect to your health. This state of uncertainty is an important, but insufficient ingredient in the development of health anxiety.

2 You experience a sense of threat to your health. When you ally this sense of threat to the sense of uncertainty mentioned above, then you will experience health anxiety, but only when you hold a set of irrational beliefs about this uncertainty-related threat.

3 As pointed out above, it is only when you hold a set of irrational beliefs about an uncertainty-related threat to your health that you will be anxious about your health. This set of beliefs includes

   (a) a rigid belief (e.g. 'I must know for sure that this spot on my arm is not malignant') and one or both of the following irrational beliefs:

   (b) an awfulizing belief (e.g. 'It is awful if I don't know that this spot on my arm is not malignant');

   (c) an LFT belief (e.g. 'I can't bear not knowing that this spot on my arm is not malignant').

4 Holding this set of beliefs about your uncertainty-related threat has three major effects:

   (a) It leads you to be anxious or worried about your health.

   (b) You tend to think that if you don't know for sure that you are OK then you are probably not (e.g. 'If I do not know for sure that this spot is benign then it is probably malignant'). Also, you will tend to seek safety by attempting to reassure yourself in your mind that the spot is benign, but as your irrational beliefs render you non-reassurable, these thinking attempts to reassure yourself bring only short-term relief.

(c) It leads to behaviour that is designed to eradicate the threat either by gaining reassurance that the threat does not exist or by avoiding thinking about the existence of the threat. Such common behaviours include:

   (i) seeking reassurance from others or from the internet that the threat does not exist. Particularly with the internet, you may end up more rather than less convinced that there is something seriously wrong with you, as such internet sites will feature remote possibilities of ill health that in your anxious state you will focus on and overemphasize in your mind;

   (ii) checking the spot frequently to see if it is getting better. If you do this by rubbing it, you will often make the spot worse and increase your anxiety as a result;

   (iii) refraining from looking at the spot on the basis of the adage 'Out of sight, out of mind'.

Needless to say, all these strategies may only bring short-term relief and do not help you deal effectively with the beliefs that underpin your uncertainty-based health anxiety. In this way, these safety-seeking manoeuvres only serve to perpetuate your problem in the longer term.

Dealing with the problem

In order to deal with uncertainty-related health anxiety, you need to address a number of factors which I will outline below. I will suggest a preferred order of dealing with these factors, but as REBT is flexible in its theory and practice, you may find that a different order works best for you. What is important is that you do deal with all the factors effectively.

Challenge your irrational beliefs about uncertainly-related health anxiety and develop alternative rational beliefs

As outlined above, health anxiety is based on a rigid demand about an uncertainly-related threat to your health and one or both of the following extreme beliefs that are derived from the rigid demand: an awfulizing belief and an LFT belief.

Responding to your rigid demand It is important that you show yourself that, while you would like to know for sure that the spot on your arm is not malignant, you don't know this at the time and you don't need to know this. I appreciate that this is easier said than done, but it is important that you recognize that your desire for certainty is fine, but your dogmatic insistence is false (just because you insist on certainty, your insistence does not create it), illogical (there is no logical connection between what exists – uncertainty – and your demand that certainty must exist) and will lead to anxiety and the thinking and behaviours (outlined above) that will maintain rather than solve the problem.

Responding to your awfulizing belief Show yourself that uncertainty about your spot being malignant is not terrible, but that it is uncomfortable, unfortunate and undesirable. If it were terrible nothing could be worse, not even your spot actually turning out to be malignant. I presume that you would admit that your spot actually being malignant is much worse than not knowing whether or not it is malignant.

Responding to your LFT belief The issue here is whether or not you can bear the uncertainty about the threat to your health or not, and whether or not it is worth bearing. It is important that you answer 'yes' to both questions. First, there is no doubt that it is a struggle putting up with not knowing whether your spot is malignant or benign, but there is a world of difference between it being a struggle and it being unbearable. The latter means that you will die or disintegrate psychologically if you face such uncertainty. Now, it is not facing this uncertain situation that leads you to feel this way: it is your LFT belief about the 'not knowing'. It is perfectly possible for you to tolerate such uncertainty if you show yourself the truth: (1) that you can tolerate it even though it is a struggle to do so; and (2) that it is worth tolerating.

In summary, if you hold the following set of rational beliefs you will feel healthily concerned about the uncertainty-related threat to your health rather than anxious about the threat:

- I would very much like to know that this spot is not malignant, but I really don't have to know this.
- It is really unfortunate not knowing that the spot is not malignant, but it is definitely not terrible.
- It's a struggle for me to put up with not knowing that the spot is not malignant, but I can tolerate this uncertainty and it is definitely worth it to me to do so.

Live in the 'Uncertainty: probably well' quadrant

What do I mean by living in the 'Uncertainty – probably well' quadrant? To answer this question, I need to explain the four quadrants that are relevant here.

Quadrant 1: 'Certainty – well' Here you know for sure that your spot is benign. Of course, this is the quadrant in which you want to live, since you are well and you don't need to seek any form of treatment. However, if your problems with uncertainty-related threats to your health are severe, then you will not believe such assurances and will think, for example, that the medical test that gave you the all-clear was wrong, and you will proceed on the basis that you are ill. If your problems are of this magnitude please see your GP and ask him or her to refer you for appropriate psychological treatment, since you need more help than I can provide you in this book.

Quadrant 2: 'Certainty – ill' Here you know for sure that your spot is malignant. It is the quadrant that you fear the most, although some people who find uncertainty intolerable say that they are relieved to know for sure that they are ill, because at least they know what it is that they are facing. If you are in this quadrant then you definitely want to seek medical treatment for your illness.

Quadrant 3: 'Uncertainty – probably ill' Here you are in a state of uncertainty, but the reality is that you are probably ill. Thus, your doctor says that your spot is probably malignant. Here it is sensible to take steps to address the problem because the signs point to you being ill.

Quadrant 4: 'Uncertainty – probably well' In this quadrant, you are in a state of uncertainty, but the evidence indicates that you are probably well. There is no clear evidence that you are ill and you are much more likely, most of the time, to be in this quadrant than you are to be in Quadrant 3.

I showed earlier that when you hold a set of irrational beliefs about an uncertainty-related threat to your health, you tend to overestimate the chances that you are ill. In our example, then, this means that if you cannot convince yourself that your spot is benign (i.e. that you are in Quadrant 1) then you think that it is malignant or that it is very probably malignant (i.e. that you are in Quadrant 3). This is why, when you hold a set of irrational beliefs, you are not comforted by favourable probabilities (i.e. being told that you are in Quadrant 4). Thus, if you are anxious because you are thinking irrationally about your uncertainty-related threat and your doctor says that he or she is 95 per cent sure that your spot is benign, then you may be reassured for a short while about what you have been told (either because you are, albeit briefly, living in Quadrant 4 or you think you are in Quadrant 1). However, once you continue to think irrationally about the threat you will convince yourself that you are in the 5 per cent malignant camp (i.e. that you are in Quadrant 3 or Quadrant 2).

In more simple terms, when you hold a set of irrational beliefs about an uncertainty-related threat to your health you have trained yourself, implicitly and unwittingly, to regard such uncertainty as inherently dangerous. What you need to do is to re-train yourself to think that uncertainty in such cases may indicate ill health, but most often is linked to good health.

There are two things that you need to do in this respect.

Manage your subsequent thinking

As we have seen, when you think irrationally about an uncertainty-related threat to your health you think in ways that are consistent with this irrational thinking. Your thoughts are consistent with living in Quadrant 3. Now, after you have challenged your irrational beliefs about the threat in ways that I discussed earlier, your subsequent thinking will still, for a time, represent you being in Quadrant 3. If you stare at an electric light for some time and then close your eyes, the after-image of the light will still be present for a while. In similar fashion, when you hold a developing rational belief after challenging its irrational counterpart, you will still have Quadrant 3 thoughts for a while.

Now for the important bit. It is important that you understand that this will happen and that your task is to recognize that such thoughts will be there and to go about your business while those thoughts are present in your mind. Do not re-engage in such thinking (e.g. by trying to reassure yourself) and do not attempt to push these thoughts out of your mind. Such re-engagement and attempts not to think the thoughts will only result in the perpetuation of these thoughts. It is as if you have tried to deal with the after-image of the light by gazing into the light again. Treat the thoughts as noise, like being aware that a radio programme is on without actively listening to it and without trying not to listen to it. Just proceed with your life while the thoughts are in your mind. You will then realize that the thoughts have gone. However, this realization will bring them back temporarily, such is the paradoxical and perverse nature of our minds! So what do you do then? Just what you did before: be aware and go about your business without re-engaging with the thoughts and without trying to get them out of your mind. You may have to do this quite a few times in any episode.

Act in ways that are consistent with your rational beliefs and inconsistent with your irrational beliefs

When you have challenged your irrational beliefs and are developing the alternatives to these beliefs, it is important that you act in ways that are consistent with these rational beliefs and inconsistent with your irrational beliefs. Now, you will probably still experience an urge to do all the things that you did when you were thinking irrationally about the threat: check the spot to see if it has changed, avoid looking at the spot and seek reassurance from professional and friends that the spot is not malignant, seek reassurance from the internet that the spot is not malignant, and so on.

The problem is not the presence of these urges. It is when you convert such an urge into an action, for example when you feel an urge to check an internet site about skin cancer to reassure yourself that your spot is benign, and you actually do so. The way to deal with such urges is similar to the way I suggested that you deal with your subsequent distorted thinking in the above section. In other words, be aware that you are experiencing the urge and don't try to get rid of it. Then I suggest that you do the opposite of your urge while rehearsing the rational belief that you have chosen to develop (see Table 4).

Table 4 Unconstructive urges and alternative constructive behaviour

Unconstructive urge	Alternative constructive behaviour
Check the spot to see if it has changed	Do not look at the spot and keep focused on the task you are doing, or begin such a task
Avoid looking at the spot	Look at the spot, rehearse your rational belief and engage in a relevant task
Seek reassurance from a professional and/or from friends that the spot is not malignant	Do not seek such reassurance or seek to reassure yourself; engage in a relevant task
Seek reassurance from the internet that the spot is not malignant	Do not seek such reassurance or seek to reassure yourself; engage in a relevant task

I have mentioned several times the importance of engaging in a relevant task as you act in ways that are consistent with your rational belief. It is important that such tasks are those that you want to engage in or that are important as part of your everyday life. I am not suggesting that you engage in such tasks as a way of distracting yourself from the urge to engage in behaviour that stems from your irrational beliefs. In fact, I actively discourage you from engaging in a task in order to distract yourself from feelings of anxiety about your uncertainty-related threat. This is because when you distract yourself, you are aiming to feel safe in the moment, which only serves to reinforce your irrational belief about the threat. When you distract yourself, it is as if you are saying: 'I need to distract myself from the threat, because if I think of it I remind myself that I can't bear to be in a state of uncertainty about my spot and if I think about it then I will conclude that the spot is malignant. Thus, it is best for me to distract myself by engaging in anything that keeps my mind off my spot.' If you feel the urge to distract yourself from your uncertainty-related threat, acknowledge the urge but use it as a cue to dispute your irrational belief, and then act in ways that are consistent with your developing rational belief.

So remember, the purpose of task-engagement should be task-engagement and not distraction.

General guidance about how to deal with uncertainty-based problems

Let me end this chapter by giving you some general advice about dealing with uncertainty-based problems.

Spell out your problem with uncertainty

This involves you doing the following:

1 Specify the situational contexts in which the problem occurs.
2 Indicate what you are most disturbed about in these situations (this is the 'A' in the ABC framework).
3 Identify the major unhealthy negative emotion that you experience about the 'A' (this is the emotional 'C' in the ABC framework).
4 List how you act or feel like acting when you experience your emotional 'C' (this is the behavioural 'C' in the ABC framework).
5 List how you think when you experience your emotional 'C' (this is known as the thinking or cognitive 'C').
6 Identify your rigid belief and your main extreme beliefs about 'A'

that explain your emotional, behavioural and thinking responses at 'C'. These beliefs occur at 'B' in the ABC framework.

State your healthy goals in dealing with such uncertainty

This involves you doing the following:

1 Specify the situational contexts in which the problem occurs. This will be the same as in (1) above.
2 Indicate what you are most disturbed about in these situations (this is the 'A' in the ABC framework and will again be the same as in (2) above).
3 Identify the major negative emotion that it would be healthy for you to experience about the 'A'. This is your emotional goal.
4 List your constructive alternative behaviours and action tendencies. This is your behavioural goal.
5 List the more realistic thinking that would accompany your new healthy negative emotion. This is your thinking goal.
6 Identify your flexible belief and your main non-extreme beliefs about 'A' that underpin your emotional, behavioural and thinking goals at 'C'.

Develop reasons why your rational beliefs are rational and your irrational beliefs are irrational

This involves you doing the following:

1 Develop reasons why your rational (i.e. flexible and non-extreme) beliefs are:
   (a) true;
   (b) logical;
   (c) productive.
2 Develop reasons why your irrational (i.e. rigid and extreme) beliefs are:
   (a) false;
   (b) illogical;
   (c) unproductive.

Act and think in ways that are consistent with your rational belief and inconsistent with your irrational belief

This involves you doing the following.

Go about your business living with uncertainty while rehearsing your rational beliefs about uncertainty

This means refraining from doing anything that is designed to rid yourself of doubt and uncertainty. Only take action when it is clear that a person who has a healthy set of beliefs about uncertainty would do so. If in doubt about this, do nothing.

Let the irrational 'voices' be

Realize that when you don't act to eradicate doubt then the part of your mind that is operating according to your set of irrational beliefs will come more to the fore. Rather than respond to each of these highly distorted thoughts, recognize where they are coming from and regard them as you would voices on the radio that you are aware of but choose not to listen to. Also, do not try not to think these thoughts. When you do practise thinking realistically to strengthen your set of rational beliefs, do so only once per episode. To do so more often is to fall prey to using such thoughts as an inappropriate source of self-reassurance, which will only maintain your problem, not deal effectively with it.

The case of Samantha

Here is how Samantha used the above schema to help her deal with her uncertainty-related problem. When reading what follows, refer back to the schema presented above where necessary.

My problem with uncertainty

- The situational contexts in which my problem occurs: *Whenever my daughter is late.*
- 'A' (what I am most disturbed about): *Not knowing that my daughter is safe.*
- 'C':
  - Emotional: *Anxiety.*
  - Behavioural: *I keep ringing her mobile to see where she is and ring her friends if I don't get any reply.*
  - Thinking: *I imagine all kinds of negative things happening to her.*
- Irrational beliefs ('B'):
  - Rigid belief: *I must know that my daughter is safe.*
  - Awfulizing belief: *It's terrible not to know that she is safe.*

My healthy goals in dealing with such uncertainty

- The situational contexts in which my problem occurs: *Whenever my daughter is late.*
- 'A' (what I want to deal with more effectively): *Not knowing that my daughter is safe.*
- My goals:
  - Emotional (the major negative emotion that it would be healthy for me to experience about the 'A'): *Concern* (rather than anxiety).
  - Behavioural (my constructive alternative behaviours and action tendencies): *Get on with whatever I am doing* (rather than keep ringing her mobile to see where she is and rather than ringing her).
  - My subsequent thinking goal (the more realistic thinking that accompanies my new healthy negative emotion): *Thinking that she is probably safe and acknowledging that despite this I will still think in a distorted way. But I will get on with things while not engaging with or trying to distract myself from such thoughts.*
- My flexible belief and main non-extreme belief about 'A' that underpin my emotional, behavioural and thinking goals at 'C':
  - Flexible belief: *I really want to know that my daughter is safe, but I don't have to have such certainty.*
  - Non-awfulizing belief: *It's bad not to know that she is safe, but it is not the end of the world.*

Reasons why my rational beliefs are rational and my irrational beliefs are irrational

It is true that I want to know for sure that my daughter is safe. This is my desire and I cannot pretend otherwise. Sadly, it is also true that I don't have to have the certainty that I want. If there were a law that I had to have this guarantee, then I would have it, which clearly I don't, so my demand that I have to know that my daughter is safe is clearly false. Also, it is clearly illogical for me to think that because I want such certainty, it must exist. My desire does not have any effect on what exists. But it is logical to note that I don't have to have what I want. This clearly makes sense. Finally, my flexible belief yields much healthier results for me than my rigid belief.

When comparing my non-extreme non-awfulizing belief with my extreme awfulizing belief, the first is clearly true, while the second is false. I can prove that it is bad if I do not know if my daughter is safe and also that it is not the end of the world if I don't have such certainty. If it were the end of the world, then nothing could be worse that not having such certainty. If this were true then it would be very strange, since it would mean that such uncertainty would be worse than the death of my daughter, which is clearly ridiculous. Also, my non-extreme belief makes sense, whereas my extreme belief does not. For when I jump from saying that it is bad not to know that my daughter is safe to saying that it is the end of the world, I am making an illogical leap in saying that something extreme follows logically from something non-extreme. Well, it doesn't. On the other hand, in my non-extreme belief, the second non-extreme component (i.e. 'it is not the end of the world not having the certainty that my daughter is safe') follows logically from the first non-extreme component (i.e. 'it is bad not knowing that my daughter is safe'). Finally, my non-extreme non-awfulizing belief also yields better results for me (emotionally, behaviourally and cognitively) than does my extreme awfulizing belief.

Actions and thoughts that are consistent with my rational belief and inconsistent with my irrational belief

When my daughter is late and I don't know that she is safe, I am going to trust her to call me if she needs to. While I will still feel the urge to call her, I am not going to act on this urge. Instead, I am going to get on with what I would be getting on with if I knew she was safe. I will briefly remind myself that uncertainty is not inherently dangerous and that she is probably safe. I am not going to do this more than once, though, otherwise I would be using this sensible thought as an unhealthy self-reassurance strategy. I still expect to have distorted thoughts about her safety. After all, I have been having such thoughts for years, but I am not going to engage with them or try to banish them from my mind. I am going to treat them as lingering reverberations from my irrational beliefs and get on with whatever activity I am involved with.

Uncertainty problems are often linked to problems with lack of control and it is the latter which I will discuss in the next chapter.

5

Dealing with lack of control

Introduction

I pointed out at the beginning of the previous chapter that it is a truism to say that we live in an uncertain world. It is also a truism to say that we are not in control of the universe! That is not to say that we have no control over what happens to us, as we obviously do, but that such control is not as great as perhaps we would like. It follows from this that we need to develop and maintain a healthy set of beliefs, particularly when we lack control over our lives and even over ourselves. Paradoxically, as I will show you later, adopting a healthy attitude to lacking control is a powerful way of gaining a sense of control.

Some of you may be familiar with the Serenity Prayer, which I have modified slightly to fit our subject of control:

> God grant me
> courage to control what I can control,
> serenity to accept what I can't control
> and wisdom to know the difference.

You will see that this prayer refers to three attitudes or qualities: courage, serenity and wisdom. I would add to this list the important ingredient of knowledge, since the whole subject of exerting control is more complicated than at first sight. So in this chapter I will discuss the healthy rational beliefs that you need to hold when you are facing adversities that are characterized by you not being in as much control as you would like.

What is control?

Control refers to the situation where you can, or 'feel' you can, bring about a direct outcome or exert some influence over something.

When we talk about control we tend to talk about being or feeling 'in control', 'not in control' or 'out of control'.

If we take being 'in control' first: this often refers to a situation where either (1) your attempts to effect a positive outcome or to prevent a negative outcome are successful; or (2) you 'feel' that these attempts will be successful.

Now, if we take the concept of not being in control, this tends to refer to the opposite of the above, i.e. a situation where either (1) your attempts to effect a positive outcome or to prevent a negative outcome are not successful; or (2) you 'feel' that these attempts will not be successful.

Finally, if we take the concept of being out of control, this often refers to the situation where you have a sense that a set of very negative outcomes are in train and you consider yourself to be powerless to do anything about them.

Control: external vs internal

It is very important to distinguish between what I call here internal control and external control. When we have, or 'feel' that we have, internal control, we are able to exert direct control (or 'feel' that we can) over those things internal to us. Here I am thinking of our behaviours, our thoughts and images, our feelings and salient aspects of our bodily and physical functioning.

When we have, or 'feel' that we have, external control, we are able to exert some influence (or 'feel' that we can) over those things external to us. Here, I am thinking of other people and aspects of our environment.

This analysis shows that, as a general rule, we have direct control (potentially, at any rate, as I will discuss presently) over ourselves, that we have influence, but not direct control, over others and that the situation is mixed with respect to aspects of our environment.

Dealing with problems with external control

In this section, I am going to address the problems where we do not have courage to exert control over what we can control or influence and where we do not have serenity to accept what we can't control externally. I will close this section by discussing the role that helplessness plays in the problems with external control.

Lack of courage to exert external control

When we lack courage to exert control over people and things external to us, we are basically in an anxious state of mind and we respond to our anxious feelings by doing nothing. We fail to act when taking action is likely to bear positive fruit. How might we explain this?

In the ABC framework, the emotional 'C' in this case is anxiety and the behavioural 'C' is failure to exert external control. 'A' is some kind of threat and 'B' is the rigid and extreme beliefs that the person holds about the threat at 'A' that account for his or her anxiety and inaction at 'C'.

What the person needs to do here, of course, is to first respond to those irrational beliefs, develop a more rational set of beliefs and act in ways that are in accord with his or her rational beliefs.

Common threats at 'A' in this regard centre on a prediction that exerted control will have a negative impact for the person (e.g. disapproval, friction between people, demotion at work, being criticized or uncertainty about the possible outcome of such exerted control).

Let me exemplify this by considering a common situation where a person does not feel in control at work as a result of not being assertive with a co-worker. Linda works at a travel agent and her colleague, Martha, gets her to do all the things that she, Martha, does not like doing. Linda meekly agrees to do this and, as a result, does not feel in control of what happens to her at work. She could assert herself and say 'no' to Martha consistently, with the result that Martha would probably eventually get the message and stop asking her to do unpleasant things for her. This would give Linda a greater sense of external control at work. However, she fears that if she takes such action there will be an unpleasant atmosphere at work between her and Martha. Here is what Linda would need to do to deal with her problem with exerting external control:

1 Identify 'C': *I am anxious and therefore do not exert control.*
2 Identify 'A': *There will be a bad atmosphere between me and Martha if I assert myself with her.*
3 Identify irrational beliefs at 'B': *Things must be harmonious between Martha and me and I couldn't bear it if there was an atmosphere between us.*
4 Challenge irrational beliefs and develop new rational beliefs at 'B': *My irrational beliefs are false, illogical and unproductive. I can put up with a bad atmosphere between Martha and myself if it comes to that, and it would be worth doing so if I can develop a better sense of control at work. And things between me and her do not have to be harmonious.*
5 Act and think in ways that are consistent with new rational beliefs: *I am going to assert myself with her from now on when she tries to get me to do the dirty work for her. Things may be awkward for a while, but they may not be.*

Lack of serenity to accept what we can't control in the external world

As every assertiveness trainer will tell you, assertiveness increases your chances of getting a positive outcome, but does not guarantee you achieving that outcome. As such, it is important that you develop the serenity to accept when you cannot bring about your desired outcome in the external world.

Let's suppose that Linda asserted herself with her colleague, Martha, but to no avail. Martha kept on trying to get Linda to do her dirty work for her, and although Linda was steadfast in her refusal, Martha kept trying. How can Linda accept the fact that she cannot successfully exert external control over Martha, meaning that Martha is impervious to Linda's assertive attempts to influence her? This is how.

Step 1   Linda recognizes that her attempts to influence Martha have not worked.

Step 2   Linda develops a set of rational, acceptance-based beliefs about her lack of control in this area. These beliefs are as follows:

(a)   *I would like Martha to stop trying to palm off her unpleasant work on me, but she does not have to do this. She is a free agent and can choose to ignore my assertive attempts to get her to stop.*

(b)   *It is bad that I cannot get Martha to stop trying to palm her work on to me, but it isn't the end of the world if she keeps doing so.*

(c)   *It is a struggle for me to put up with not being able to get Martha to stop trying to palm her unpleasant tasks on to me, but I can tolerate this and it is worth it to me to do so since it will help me to stay in employment until I am able to get a better job.*

(d)   *While this aspect of life is bad, the whole of life is not bad. It is a complex mixture of positive, negative (including this one) and neutral aspects.*

Step 3   Linda gets on with her life while acting and thinking in ways consistent with her rational beliefs. Having developed her set of acceptance-based rational beliefs about her lack of external control or, more strictly speaking, influence over Martha's behaviour, Linda continues with her life at work and at home. She does not dwell on her lack of external control. Rather, Linda reminds herself that while she cannot influence Martha to stop her behaviour, she still has internal control in the sense that she can say 'no' to Martha every time she tries to get Linda to do mundane tasks for her.

This latter point is very important. It is really the essence of the serenity part of the Serenity Prayer. For, when you adopt a set of rational beliefs about what you cannot control in the external world, you are developing a powerful sense of what you can control in the internal world. This is the value of acceptance. It may not give you serenity, but you do not disturb yourself about your lack of external control and therefore you can move on with your life.

Helplessness and the need to exert external control

When you believe that you have to exert control over your external environment and your efforts are unsuccessful, then you may experience a sense of helplessness and feel depressed. If you have the kind of personality where you value autonomy and you are rigid about being autonomous, then this will be problematic for you for two reasons. First, you may give up all attempts to exert external control when such efforts may prove successful. Second, you may focus on your helplessness-based depression and further depress yourself about this. If you are autonomous in your personality organization – and even if you are not – it is important that you develop the following rational beliefs about external control:

> I would like to exert external control, but I do not have to do so. If my attempts are unsuccessful, that is unfortunate but not the end of the world and I am not a helpless individual. I am a person who can control what I can control externally and who can accept, but not like, what I cannot control in my environment. If I develop this idea I will have internal control about not having external control.

Dealing with problems with internal control

When we experience problems with internal control, we are unable (or 'feel' we are unable) to control one of our internal processes such as our behaviour, our thinking or our feelings, to name but three. There are two problems here. First, we may be using a commonsense but ineffective way of bringing about internal control, and second, we may disturb ourselves about our loss of internal control.

Let me begin with the second issue and discuss how we disturb ourselves about losing internal control and what we can do about this.

As I said above, we can disturb ourselves when we lose control of our behaviour, our thinking and our emotions. Let me deal with these one at time.

Self-disturbance about losing behavioural control

I made the point in Chapter 1 when considering behaviour that there is a distinction between an urge to act (or what is often called an action tendency) and overt behaviour. Thus, you may feel the urge to punch someone in the face, but normally you will not act on that urge. Thus, when we disturb ourselves about loss of behavioural control we can do so when that loss is characterized by overt behaviour or when an action tendency is experienced as loss of behavioural control. Here is an example.

> Bernard was shopping in an up-market department store in London for his wife's birthday. After he had bought what he was looking for, he decided to browse in the store for a while. While browsing, Bernard saw a watch that he had always wanted, but which was well out of his price range. Suddenly, Bernard felt a very strong urge to steal the watch. He reacted to this with acute anxiety and ran out of the store. Subsequently, he avoided going anywhere near the store and would come out in a cold sweat at the mere mention of the store's name.

Using the ABC framework, let's see if we can understand Bernard's reaction.

A = *I experienced a strong urge to steal a watch in the store which is evidence that I was losing control of myself.*

B = *'I must not lose control and it is awful that I am doing so.'*

C (emotional) = *Anxiety.*
(behavioural) = *Withdrawal and later avoidance of store and the surrounding area.*
(thinking) = *'I would have stolen the watch if I had remained in the store. I have no control over such urges.'*

Please note one very important point. Bernard's irrational belief about his loss of self-control (as he construed his urge to take the watch) led not only to a disturbed emotional reaction and unconstructive behavioural reaction at 'C', but also to a distorted thinking response at 'C'. I discussed the thinking consequences of irrational and rational beliefs on pp. 8–13 in Chapter 1 and I refer you to that material for full coverage of this point.

In Bernard's case, his irrational belief led him to conclude that if he stayed in the store the experience of the urge would have inevitably led him to steal the watch. He thus concluded that he had no control when he experienced his urges. Note here the impact of Bernard's irrational beliefs on his subsequent distorted thinking. The content of this thinking reveals Bernard's conviction that he will lose all control (i.e. he will steal the watch) if he loses some control (i.e. when he experiences an unwanted urge). Thus, irrational beliefs about some loss of control create the idea in your mind that you will lose all control if you do not take measures to prevent this from happening. In Bernard's case this meant withdrawing immediately from the store and later avoiding the store itself and the surrounding area. But why should Bernard avoid the area surrounding the store?

The answer to this question reveals something important about 'loss of control' fears. Bernard avoids this area because being there reminds him of his 'loss of control' experience and he wants to escape these thoughts. Thus, Bernard is not only afraid of losing control of his behaviour should he return to the department store: he is scared of the thoughts he would get should he return to that area.

Bernard has to do the following in order to deal with his fear of loss of behavioural control.

1   He needs to challenge his irrational beliefs and develop an alternative set of rational beliefs: *'Even if having the urge to steal the watch is evidence that I am not in as much control of my behaviour as I would like to be, I don't have to be in that much control, and beginning to lose control in the way that I did is bad but not awful.'*

2   He needs to act and think in ways that are consistent with this developing rational belief: *Bernard needs to return to the department store and experience his urge to steal the watch while rehearsing his rational belief. If he stays in the situation, Bernard will realize that an urge to steal when 'de-awfulized' does not inevitably lead to the act of stealing, and that when a little loss of control is processed with a flexible belief rather than a rigid one it remains just that – a little loss of control – and does not lead to total loss of control, which is what Bernard thought would happen when he rigidly processed his urge to steal.*

If Bernard thinks that doing this would be too much too soon, he might start by rehearsing the following rational belief as he approaches the area close to the department store: 'I would rather not think about what happened when I was in the department store, but that does not mean that I must not have these thoughts. I can bear having these thoughts.' If Bernard thought like this he would not be frightened of thinking about his urge to steal and would not have to avoid the store or its surrounding area, since the reason he was avoiding them in the first place was to avoid the thoughts he predicted he would have while in this area.

Self-disturbance about losing control of one's thinking

I have alluded to how to deal with losing thinking control when discussing Bernard's case, but let me now do so more thoroughly. One of the design features of being human, in my view, is that we do not have perfect control over the way we think. People who meditate, even those who are expert at it, will tell you that when they focus on their particular mantra, all kinds of thoughts come into their mind which take them away from their focus. Part of meditation therefore is to understand that non-mantra thoughts will come into your mind, and the important thing is the stance that you take to these irrelevant thoughts. There are basically four such stances.

1 Try to banish the thoughts from your mind.
2 Engage with these thoughts.
3 Accept the existence of these thoughts and let them be, without engagement and attempts at banishment.
4 Repeat the thoughts until you get bored with them.

People who meditate a lot learn to implement the third stance, and I will return to this issue later.

When you have a thought, way of thinking or mental image and you disturb yourself about it, then you are doing so because you are holding a set of irrational beliefs about your thinking.

Here is an example. Lois went to visit Jane, her best friend, who had just had a baby. They were talking in Jane's kitchen and Lois was cutting up an onion with a knife when she had the thought, 'What would it be like to stab Jane's baby?' There was no urge attached to the thought (as happened with Bernard above), but Lois was appalled by it, excused herself because she said she felt ill and went home. Subsequently, she avoided all contact with Jane and refused to touch sharp knives. As we will now see, Lois had two problems about her thought. I will outline each problem and then show what Lois would need to do in order to address each one effectively.

Problem 1: Fear of doing harm

A = *I thought what it would be like to stab Jane's baby. This is an alien thought that means that I am beginning to lose control of my thinking.*
B = *'I must be in complete control of my thinking and it is terrible not to be so.'*

C   (emotional) = *Anxiety*.

(behavioural) = *Avoidance (of Jane, sharp knives and babies)*.

(thinking) = *'If I think this way I will harm Jane's baby and other babies as well.' 'I won't have a baby myself in case I harm it.'*

What follows is Lois's new ABC once she had challenged and changed her irrational beliefs:

A = *I thought what it would be like to stab Jane's baby. This is an alien thought that means I am beginning to lose control of my thinking.*

B = *'I prefer to be in complete control of my thinking, but I do not have to be. Having alien thoughts that I can't control is unpleasant and unwanted, but not terrible.'*

C   (emotional) = *Concern*.

(behavioural) = *Going to see Jane and her baby; approaching other babies; holding sharp knives.*

(thinking) = *'Having such thoughts is evidence of the paradoxical nature of mind and not evidence that I will harm Jane's baby and other babies. I will have a baby if I want to have one. I have no evidence that I will harm it.'*

Problem 2: Shame of not being in control of one's thinking

A = *I thought what it would be like to stab Jane's baby. This is an alien thought that means that I have a defect because I can't control my thinking.*

B = *'I must not have this defect and I am defective because I do.'*

C   (emotional) = *Shame*.

(behavioural) = *Avoidance (of Jane, sharp knives and babies)*.

(thinking) = *'People will think I'm a freak if they find out about what I thought.'*

What follows is Lois's new ABC once she had challenged and changed her irrational beliefs:

A = *I thought what it would be like to stab Jane's baby. This is an alien thought that means that I have a defect because I can't control my thinking.*

B = *'If I have a defect, I am not a defective person, but a fallible human being who had a weird thought that she could not control. I don't have to be free of such a defect.'*

C   (emotional) = *Disappointment*.

(behavioural) = *Going to see Jane and her baby; approaching other babies; holding sharp knives.*

(thinking) = *'I will get a mixed response if people find out about what I thought. Some will think I'm a freak, but others won't.'*

Self-disturbance about losing emotional control

Our beliefs about our emotions determine how much in control we 'feel' when we experience them. While we may put a rein on positive emotions because we fear losing control if we feel them, it is more the negative emotions we fear for risk of losing internal control.

In particular, we are more likely to 'feel' that we are losing internal control when we experience anger and anxiety.

Anger

If you fear experiencing anger because you think you will lose internal control as a result, then you hold an irrational belief about this feeling. You may believe that you must not feel anger and that if you do, terrible things will happen – for example, you will become very aggressive and run amok. As a result, you avoid confrontations where you are likely to feel anger and may overcompensate by being excessively nice to the person that you are angry with.

To address this problem, you need to show yourself that while you may not want to be angry, there is no reason why you have to be immune from experiencing it. Once you allow yourself to experience anger and also learn how to assert yourself with the person you are angry with, then you will fear it less.

Anxiety

Many people fear anxiety, and because they believe that they must gain control of this emotion immediately, they only become more anxious rather than less. This is because the very feeling of anxiety becomes a threat to them and they respond to this threat with increased anxiety. In addition, because anxiety has a variety of physical symptoms like heart palpitations, if you do not understand this you may end up by thinking that you are having a heart attack, and consequently you may have a panic attack.

Dealing with anxiety when it is a trigger for fearing losing internal control involves you doing a number of things.

- First, as elsewhere you need to be flexible and not rigid about experiencing anxiety. If you believe that you would rather not be anxious but that you don't have to get rid of this feeling, and if you prove to yourself that anxiety is a painful but bearable emotion, then you will begin the process of developing a sense of internal control in response to being anxious.

- Second, you need to show yourself that experiencing anxiety is unfortunate, but hardly the end of the world. It is a painful emotion, to be sure, but not an unbearable one, and if you see also that it is worth bearing (since bearing anxiety allows you to deal constructively with threat rather than avoid it), then these attitudes will also help you to restore a sense of control in the face of anxiety.

Western, Eastern and paradoxical approaches to losing internal control

Dealing with your irrational beliefs about losing internal control is perhaps the most important thing you can do to regain a greater sense of internal control. While there are a number of strategies designed to promote such control, none of them will help you in the longer term as long as you are disturbing yourself about losing internal control. So before you implement these strategies, first identify, challenge and change the irrational beliefs that underpin your self-disturbance about losing internal control and develop their rational belief alternatives.

I distinguish between Western, Eastern and paradoxical approaches to regaining internal control. The Western approach to regaining internal control is based on the idea that you need to do something in order to regain internal control. Once you have done this and it works, you will have regained a sense of internal control.

By contrast, the Eastern approach is based on the idea of not doing anything when you feel out of control. Rather, you acknowledge and accept whatever it is that you are experiencing. While the Western approach is explicit in stating that the application of certain techniques is designed to yield a greater sense of internal control, with the Eastern approach this design is more implicit. Otherwise, what is the point of adopting a 'do nothing, acceptance-based' approach if it is not designed to bring about the same result as with the Western approach?

Finally, the paradoxical approach to gaining internal control is counter-intuitive. It involves you doing the reverse of what your common sense tells you to do. Thus, if you have an intrusive, unwanted thought, your common sense tells you to get rid of it. By contrast, the paradoxical approach encourages you to repeat the thought many times until you get used to it or bored with it and it therefore loses its disturbed sting, as it were.

Let's consider the Eastern approach to gaining internal control.

The Eastern approach: thinking

A well-known psychology experiment showed that when you ask people to think about a white polar bear and then instruct them not to think about it, then these people report that this instruction does not work. Trying not to think something is not an effective strategy.

So if you have a thought that is alien to you, an intrusive thought that you would rather not have, then trying not to have this thought just won't work. Instead, a better strategy, based on the Eastern approach, is to acknowledge the existence of the thought, and that's it! Here, it is important not to engage with the thought (for example, to reassure yourself that the thought is not dangerous), to eradicate the thought or to distract yourself from the thought. Once you have acknowledged the existence of the thought, then it is important that you get on with whatever you would have been doing if you had not had the thought. If you do this you will become aware that you are not thinking the thought. This awareness will bring the thought back into your mind. The best way of responding to this is to do what you did before: accept the thought and then get on with life.

The Eastern approach: emotions

The Eastern approach to emotions is again to acknowledge that you are feeling a certain way and then to do nothing to get rid of this feeling or to engage with it. This approach is based on the idea that all emotions, whether they are healthy or unhealthy, are part of the human experience, and it is not the feelings themselves that pose a problem to us. Rather, it is how we tend to respond to these feelings. In particular, our attempts to stop the experience are regarded, within the Eastern approach, as particularly problematic.

The Eastern approach: behaviour

As I pointed out in Chapter 1, when we consider behaviour we need to distinguish between overt behaviour and action tendencies (or urges to act). The Eastern approach to behaviour is as follows.

Overt behaviour The Eastern approach to behaviour recommends that when you have acted in a way that is unconstructive, your response is to acknowledge and accept that you acted in this way. This stance is intended to prevent you from disturbing yourself about the way you acted and will help you to reflect on the reasons you acted in the way you did. My own view is that you will be able to do this if your beliefs about your behaviour are rational, but not if they are irrational.

Action tendencies The Eastern approach to action tendencies is again to acknowledge and to accept that you have such urges, and therefore you have neither to act on them nor to eradicate them. Again, this is good advice as long as your beliefs about these urges are rational.

The Western approach to gaining internal control

This book is largely based on the Western approach to gaining control, although, as you can tell, it incorporates the Eastern approach to the acceptance of experience.

The Western approach taken in this book is based on the idea that when you experience a disturbed emotion or an unconstructive behaviour or action tendency, you can deal with these responses as follows. First you need to assess what you are most disturbed about and then identify the irrational beliefs that underpin your disturbed response. You can help yourself by challenging these beliefs and developing rational alternatives to these beliefs. Then, you need to act on these beliefs and accept that your disturbed feelings, distorted thoughts and urges to act in unconstructive ways will not change until you have implemented your rational belief and have acted in ways that strengthen them over time. How long does this process take? It takes as long as it takes until your beliefs are rational and impact constructively on your feelings, behaviour and subsequent thinking. When you have achieved this you will have gained an enduring sense of internal control.

The paradoxical approach to gaining internal control

As I suggested above, the paradoxical approach to gaining internal control urges you to repeat something until you get bored with it and it loses its disturbability. For example, Dennis had the thought that he might stab his girlfriend while they were watching TV. Using the paradoxical approach to gaining internal control, he passed a sharp knife across the neck of his girlfriend (with her informed consent) many times until he got bored with it.

Frances, a religious woman who thought about having sex with Jesus and hence avoided all things religious, helped herself to gain a sense of control over her thoughts by repeating to herself many times, 'I want to have sex with Jesus.' She did so until she became thoroughly bored with this thought and thus gained a sense of internal control over her thinking.

Having outlined these three approaches to gaining internal control, I invite you to use the approach which you think will help you the most.

Use it and evaluate its results. If it works for you, use it. If not, experiment with one or both of the other approaches.

My own opinion on this issue is that if you are disturbing yourself about not having as much external or internal control as you would like, deal with the underlying irrational beliefs as outlined in the Western approach to gaining control. Then, use the Eastern or the paradoxical approach until you feel in greater control of yourself and the controllable aspects of the world around you.

The need to exert internal control and fear of losing complete control

When you believe that you have to exert control over your internal processes and your efforts are unsuccessful, then you may experience a sense of anxiety, bordering on panic. If you have the kind of personality where internal control is valued and you are rigid about being in control of yourself, then this will be problematic for you for the following reason. You may fear losing complete control of yourself and perhaps even going mad. Such a fear is known as phrenophobia and particularly occurs in people who are rigid about internal control and for whom a little loss of internal control means that a complete loss of internal control is imminent.

If you are rigid about internal control, it is important that you develop the following rational beliefs about internal control:

> I would like to exert internal control, but I do not have to do so. If my attempts are unsuccessful that is unfortunate but not the end of the world and I am not about to lose complete internal control. If I develop this idea I will have internal control about not having internal control!

Problems with uncertainty and lack of control often co-exist

In the previous chapter, I discussed problems that people have with uncertainty. I made the point in that chapter that people tend only to have problems with uncertainty when it is linked with other problems. One very common problematic combination occurs when your need for certainty is linked with your need for control. Thus, you believe, for example, that you have to know now that you will be in control later, and if you don't know this now then you will lose control later. This applies to both external control and internal control.

In order to deal with these linked demands you need to challenge them separately and develop a linked set of rational beliefs, namely, 'I would like to know now that I will be in control later, but I don't have to know this.' Such a rational belief will help you to live in the healthy quadrant, where you don't know now that you will be in control later, but the probability is that you will be in control. If you act and think accordingly you will help yourself enormously, especially if you do this over time.

In the next chapter I will consider how best to deal with failure.

6

Dealing with failure

Introduction

A number of years ago, I was consulted by a young man with an unusual story. The young man, whom I will call Kevin, told me the following:

Kevin: I have been asked to come and see you, but there is nothing you can do for me. I am only here to satisfy my parents.

Dr Dryden: OK, so why don't you tell me why they want you to see me.

Kevin: Because I am going to kill myself. Let me tell you the story. I have just been awarded a double first from Oxford in Physics. If I work reasonably hard I will get a PhD and probably join the teaching staff, and if I work really hard there is a reasonably good chance that I will be awarded a Nobel Prize for Physics.

Dr Dryden: So why do you want to kill yourself?

Kevin: Because Linus Pauling has two Nobel Prizes and, no matter how hard I work, I will never get two Nobel Prizes, so I am going to kill myself because I am an abject failure.

I did not engage Kevin in therapy. He did his duty to his parents by consulting me for one session and I never saw or heard from him again. So, I don't know if he is alive or dead.

What this episode clearly shows is that it is not our objective achievements or the lack of them that determine our reactions, but again it is our beliefs about these achievements (or their lack) that largely influence the way we feel, behave and think.

What, then, could Kevin's beliefs be that led him to consider suicide when, even at his own admission, he had a glittering future ahead of him? We did not get far enough to discuss his beliefs, but my hunch is that Kevin's beliefs were rigid and extreme. So here is my version of his ABC.

A (what Kevin was most disturbed about) = *Not being able to achieve at least what Linus Pauling has achieved.*

B (Kevin's irrational beliefs) = *'I must be able to achieve what Linus Pauling achieved and I am an abject failure because I can't do so.'*

C (emotional) = *Depression.*
(behaviour) = *Suicidal behaviour.*
(thinking) = *'I see no hope for myself since I cannot match Linus Pauling's achievements.'*

In this chapter, I will discuss the six most common problems that people have with failure:

1 demanding that one must succeed and thinking of oneself as a failure if one fails;
2 feeling shame for bringing shame on one's reference group because of one's failure;
3 feeling guilty about hurting people's feelings by one's failure;
4 failure and competitiveness;
5 failure and not being in control of one's fate;
6 failure and struggling with harsher conditions.

I will deal with each of these problems in turn.

Dealing with failure-related demands and self-depreciation

The problem

When you make rigid demands on yourself with respect to your performance and you fail, you also tend to think that your failure defines you. I call this the performance–identity problem. When you don't achieve the level of performance or achievement that you demand of yourself, two things happen. First, you think you have failed, and second, you think of yourself as a failure for failing.

For example, Tamara was a fantastic gymnast, but had just failed narrowly to get into the national gymnastics team. Her rigid belief was that she had to get into the team and that because she did not she was no good as a gymnast and useless as a person.

Dealing with the problem

Many people tried to convince Tamara that she had done very well even to be considered for the national team. Objectively, Tamara had made rapid progress in a short period of time; however, she was not reacting to the objective facts, but to her rigid and self-depreciating beliefs about her failure to get into the team.

In short, you do not help people deal with their disturbance over failing by trying to show them that what they consider to be their failures are, in fact, successes.

Rather, you need to take a very different tack. So if you are disturbing yourself about failure, what can you do to help yourself?

Step 1	Assume temporarily that you have failed.
Step 2	Identify your disturbed reactions to this failure.
Step 3	Identify the irrational beliefs that underpin your disturbance.
Step 4	Challenge these irrational beliefs and develop an alternative set of rational beliefs.
Step 5	Act and think according to your rational beliefs.
Step 6	Develop a more compassionate view of success and failure.

Let's see how Tamara used the above schema to help herself.

Step 1	Assume temporarily that you have failed: *'My failure to get into the national gymnastics team constitutes failure.'*
Step 2	Identify your disturbed reactions to this failure: *'I feel depressed about this and want to give up gymnastics.'*
Step 3	Identify the irrational beliefs that underpin your disturbance: *'I must not fail and I am a failure because I did.'*
Step 4	Challenge these irrational beliefs and develop an alternative set of rational beliefs: *'I would like to have succeeded by getting into the national gymnastics team, but sadly there is no law that dictates that I must get what I want. The fact that I did not get into the team is a failure from one perspective, but I am never a failure for falling short of my goals. I am far too complex to be defined by this failure. I am a very complex human being who may have failed in this respect, but I have succeeded in many other respects, including getting so close to selection.'*
Step 5	Act and think according to your rational beliefs: *'If I give up gymnastics then I will have not fulfilled my potential. So I will continue to train and perform and strive to do the best I can and see if I will be selected next time.'*
Step 6	Develop a more compassionate view of success and failure: *'Now that I can see that I did not have to be selected for the team and that I am not a failure as a person for failing to be selected, I can stand back and see that getting so far in such a short period of time is quite an achievement.'*

Dealing with feelings of shame for bringing shame on one's reference group for having failed

The problem

When you think you have brought shame on your reference group for having failed and you feel shame for doing so, a number of factors are involved.

1 Your reference group is a tightly knit group which prides itself on success.
2 If one member of that reference group fails then it reflects badly on that reference group, as judged by the reference group itself and by the wider community with which the reference group is connected.
3 The member who has failed experiences shame for being the source of shame for the reference group, because he or she holds a set of irrational beliefs about this. For example, the person believes, 'I absolutely should not have let the reference group down and I am defective for doing so.'
4 The person acts in a way that is consistent with the irrational beliefs that underpin his or her shame. This usually involves the person trying to hide the failure or, if this is impossible, leaving the reference group in an attempt to spare the reference group the shame of his or her continued presence.

Let's see how this applies to Geoff, who came from a long line of distinguished doctors. The family was well respected by the wider medical community, in which the family members mixed, and prided itself on its reputation. In particular, male members of the family were expected to carry on the family tradition of medical distinction.

Thus, Geoff was expected to become a distinguished doctor and sincerely wanted to be a source of pride for his family. Unfortunately, Geoff had little talent for medicine and, despite working hard, failed his first year exams so badly that he was strongly advised to leave medical school on the basis of his poor results.

Using the above schema, let's understand the factors involved in Geoff's shame about his failure and being a source of shame, not pride, for his family.

1 Geoff's family is his reference group and it is a tightly knit group which prides itself on medical success.
2 Geoff's failure would reflect badly on his family, as judged by the family itself and by the wider medical community.
3 Geoff experiences shame for being the source of shame for his

family. He believes the following: 'I absolutely should not have failed my medical exams and brought shame on my family and I am a defective person for doing so.'

4 Because of his feelings of shame, Geoff cannot face his family to tell them in person that he failed and was asked to leave medical school. So he tells them in a note and leaves the country to go to work on a remote kibbutz in Israel.

Dealing with the problem

In order to deal with the shame of bringing shame on your reference group by your failure, you would have to do the following:

1 Admit that your failure reflects badly on your reference group as judged by the reference group itself and by the wider community with which the reference group is connected.

2 Admit that you feel shame about this and identify the irrational beliefs that underpin this experience of shame.

3 Challenge and change these irrational beliefs and develop an alternative set of rational beliefs: for example, show yourself that you would have preferred not to have let your reference group down, but that does not mean that it absolutely should not happen. Additionally, acknowledge that you are not defective for doing so. Rather, you are a fallible human being whose failure in this respect has had such a negative outcome for yourself and your reference group. These rational beliefs will lead you to feel disappointment rather than shame for your failure and for bringing shame on your reference group.

4 Act in a way that is consistent with your rational beliefs that underpin your disappointment. This usually involves staying to face up to your failure and your reference group, with your head held high.

This is how Geoff used the above schema to effectively address his shame-based problem with failure and how it reflected on his family.

1 Geoff admitted that his failure reflected badly on his family as judged by his family itself and by the wider medical community.

2 Geoff admitted that he feels shame about this and identified the following irrational beliefs that underpinned his experience of shame: *'I absolutely should not have failed my medical exams and brought shame on my family and I am a defective person for doing so.'*

3 Geoff challenged and changed these irrational beliefs and developed an alternative set of rational beliefs, namely: *'I would have preferred*

not to have let my family down by failing my medical exams, but that does not mean that it absolutely should not have happened. I am not a defective person for doing so. Rather, I am a fallible human being for failing and for bringing shame on my family.'

As a result, he felt disappointment rather than shame for both of these things.

4 Geoff acted in the following ways which were consistent with his developing rational beliefs: *Geoff told his family face to face that he had failed his medical exams, that the academic authorities would not take him back and that he was going to stay and find an alternative career. He did this with his head held high, despite the distress and shame his family experienced.*

Dealing with feelings of guilt for hurting people's feelings by one's failure

The problem

While guilt and shame both stem from a rigid demand and both involve self-depreciation, they differ in a number of ways. When you feel shame in the context of failure, you are usually focused on falling very short of your ideals and on the impact that this has on how your reference group views itself and how it is viewed by the wider community. Also, the content of your self-depreciation in shame centres on there being something wrong with you (e.g. 'I'm defective').

On the other hand, when you experience guilt in the context of failure you feel guilty about the hurt you think you have caused others, and the content of your self-depreciation is that you are bad.

Geoff (whom we met in the previous section) also experienced a feeling of guilt for hurting his family's feelings as result of his failure. This is Geoff's ABC:

A = *I hurt my family's feelings by failing my medical exam.*
B = *'I absolutely should not have hurt their feelings and I am a bad person for doing so.'*
C (emotional) = *Guilt.*
(behavioural) = *Begging my family for forgiveness; depriving myself of pleasure.*
(thinking) = *'I need to be punished for this.'*

Here is how Geoff dealt with his feelings of guilt and felt remorse instead:

A = *I hurt my family's feelings by failing my medical exams.*

B = '*I wish I had not hurt my family's feelings, but I am not, and nor do I have to be, immune from doing so. I am not a bad person for doing so. I am a fallible human being who has done a bad thing.*'

C (emotional) = *Remorse.*

(behavioural) = *Saying sorry to my family without begging for forgiveness; involving myself in pleasurable pursuits.*

(thinking) = '*I do not need to be punished for this. My family contribute to their hurt feelings by their beliefs about me becoming a doctor.*'

Dealing with failure and competitiveness

The problem

If we revisit the case of Kevin, whose story I discussed at the beginning of the chapter, it is apparent that it is basically a story of failure and competitiveness, albeit an unusual one. Kevin considered that he was in competition with Linus Pauling. He further believed that he had to match Linus Pauling, and considered himself an abject failure because he concluded that he could not do so.

There is nothing intrinsically wrong with competition. In fact, it can urge people to achieve things that they probably would not achieve in a non-competitive environment. However, it is important to differentiate between two different types of competitiveness: healthy competitiveness and unhealthy competitiveness.

In healthy competitiveness, you identify someone whom you see as a rival in some way and you hold the following rational beliefs: 'I want to beat or equal the performance of my rival, but I don't have to do so. If I don't that would be very unfortunate, but as my identity is not defined by my performance, I can accept myself as a fallible human being who can still strive to be the best that I can be, even though my rival may achieve better.'

In unhealthy competitiveness, you again identify someone whom you see as a rival in some way, but this time you hold the following irrational beliefs: 'I must beat or equal the performance of my rival. If I don't I am a failure.'

Dealing with the problem

So it is clear that Kevin experienced unhealthy competitiveness with Linus Pauling. This is what he would need to do to be healthily competitive with his rival, Linus Pauling.

First and foremost, he would need to challenge and change his irrational beliefs to rational beliefs. If you recall, Kevin's irrational beliefs were: 'I must be able to achieve what Linus Pauling achieved and I am an abject failure because I can't do so.'

If he were to challenge the rigid part of this belief, Kevin would need to acknowledge that there is no law of nature that decrees that he would have to achieve what Linus Pauling achieved. If there was such a law, then he would have to match Linus Pauling's achievements. Indeed, he would have no choice but to do so.

Then, if he were to challenge the self-depreciation part of his belief, he would assert that his 'self' was far too complex to be equated by his presumed failure to be awarded two Nobel Prizes.

His new flexible and non-extreme beliefs would be: 'I would very much like to be able to achieve what Linus Pauling has achieved, but I certainly do not have to do so. If I fail to match his achievement, I have failed in that regard, but I am definitely not an abject failure. I am fallible, and I am going to see what I can achieve rather than kill myself.'

Kevin's new rational beliefs would help him to see just how close he could get to matching Linus Pauling's achievements. As such, the competitiveness Kevin would experience would be healthy in nature and encourage him to actualize his own potential rather than replicate Linus Pauling's potential. However, if Kevin kept his irrational beliefs, then his unhealthy competitiveness would not just lead to hopelessness: it would also, in his case, be life-threatening.

Dealing with failure and not being in control of one's fate

One of the main points of this book is not to take issues too much at face value. Thus, it may be that your main problem with failure is failure itself – but it may not be. As we have seen, you may be more preoccupied with the shame that you may be bringing on your reference group, with hurting other people's feelings or with losing out to a rival.

The problem

Another common problem that people have with failure is the loss of control over their fate that they infer failure means. Note how, in this problem, the focus of the current chapter (i.e. failure) is linked with the topic of the previous chapter (i.e. control).

Let me give you an example of where failure means lack of control over one's fate.

Roger was referred to me because he was depressed over his failure to get promoted at work. In discussing his problem, I found out that Roger did not regard himself as a failure. Rather, like Kevin, who I discussed at the beginning of the chapter, Roger had a positive view of himself which was not shaken by his failure to be promoted.

This is how the ensuing dialogue went.

Dr Dryden:	So you are not depressed about your failure to get promoted because you think of yourself as a failure?
Roger:	That's right. I am more depressed because my plan has been spoilt.
Dr Dryden:	Your plan?
Roger:	Yes: I made a plan about five years ago about where I wanted to be in ten years, and it was all going well until I failed to get that promotion.
Dr Dryden:	So you are depressed about your plan being spoilt?
Roger:	Yes, it means that I am no longer in control over what happens to me and I find that very depressing.

Let me put Roger's situation into the ABC framework and show how I helped him to deal with the failure-related fate control problem.

A = *I don't have control over my fate.*
B = *'I must have control over my fate and I can't stand it when I don't.'*
C (emotional) = *Depression.*
  (behavioural) = *Stay off work.*
  (thinking) = *'I am helpless.'*

Dealing with the problem

I helped Roger to question and change his irrational beliefs and helped him to develop an alternative set of rational beliefs, as follows:

A = *I don't have control over my fate.*

B = *'I would like to have control over my fate, but since I don't run the universe I don't have to have this. I can stand it when I don't, although it is difficult.'*

C (emotional) = *Sadness.*

(behavioural) = *Stay in work and retry for promotion.*

(thinking) = *'I may not have complete control over things, but there is a lot that I can control, like my own responses when my fate is taken out of my hands.'*

People like Roger are highly autonomous in their personality organization and thrive on being in control, effective and independent. If they fail to get these conditions met, they are vulnerable to disturbing themselves, but only when they hold rigid and extreme beliefs about the presence of their preferred autonomous conditions. This is why it is so important that they learn to be flexible and non-extreme about the absence of these conditions. For, while they cannot change their personality, they decidedly can learn to take a flexible and non-extreme stance to obstacles to autonomy, such as when they fail in some way. This is what Roger did and what you can do if this applies to you.

Dealing with problems of struggling with the hardship that comes with failure

The problem

In the previous section, I discussed what happens when failure for the person means the absence of autonomy. It also happens that the reason people disturb themselves about failure is again not because they have failed *per se*, but because their failure leads to greater hardship in their lives, and it is the resulting hardship that they disturb themselves about. This is what happened to Fiona. Here is her story.

> Fiona was unemployed and set her heart on getting a job at the local supermarket, which would have meant that she would have some money to spend on entertainment, and thus have some fun in her life. Unfortunately, Fiona failed to get the job and disturbed herself about her failure. What Fiona was most disturbed about with respect to her failure to get the supermarket job was that this meant that she would be faced with continued hardship and she would not have money to have fun.

When you disturb yourself about the presence of hardship in your life that follows failure, you are doing the following:

1 You focus on the hardship that failure brings.
2 You bring to this hardship a set of irrational (i.e. rigid and extreme) beliefs.
3 You experience a set of unhealthy emotional, behavioural and thinking consequences of these beliefs that actually give you the additional hardship of disturbance to deal with. Thus you have two hardships for the price of one!
4 Such disturbed reactions impede rather than facilitate a constructive approach to dealing with the environmental hardship.

Let me outline Fiona's ABC:

A = *Continued hardship brought about by my failure to get the supermarket job.*
B = *'I must not have continued hardship in my life and I can't stand the fact that this is happening.'*
C (emotional) = *Depression.*
(behavioural) = *Stop applying for jobs.*
(thinking) = *'I will never get out of this situation.'*

Dealing with the problem

Having outlined the problem, let me show how you can deal with it.

1 You again focus on the hardship that failure brings.
2 You challenge and change your irrational (i.e. rigid and extreme) beliefs and develop an alternative rational (i.e. flexible and non-extreme) set of beliefs.
3 You experience a set of healthy emotional, behavioural and thinking consequences of these rational beliefs that do not add to the hardship you are facing at 'A'.
4 Such healthy reactions facilitate rather than impede a constructive approach to dealing with the environmental hardship.

Let me outline Fiona's new ABC which, as you will see, helped her to address the hardship that stemmed from her failure.

A = *Continued hardship brought about by my failure to get the supermarket job.*
B = *'I would rather not have continued hardship in my life, but sadly it does not have to be the way I want it to be. I will struggle with this, but I can stand it and it's worth standing because doing so will help me get a job, and some money for fun, in the longer term.'*

C (emotional) = *Disappointment.*
   (behavioural) = *Continue to apply for jobs.*
   (thinking) = *'Getting out of this situation will be difficult, but there is no evidence that I will never get out of it.'*

Having showed you how to deal with failure and its vicissitudes, I will turn my attention to helping you deal effectively with disapproval and rejection in the next chapter.

7

Dealing with disapproval and rejection

Introduction

Generally, when we are approved or accepted by people that we care about, we tend to have very positive feelings about the presence of these highly desirable conditions. It follows, then, that when we are disapproved or rejected by these same people, this constitutes an adversity for us.

In this chapter, I will cover the following issues that concern disapproval and rejection.

1 When you disturb yourself about disapproval or rejection *per se*.
2 When disapproval or rejection means to you that you won't be looked after and you disturb yourself about this.
3 When disapproval or rejection means to you that you will lose advantages and you disturb yourself about this.
4 When you overestimate disapproval and rejection and attempt to prevent them from happening.

While disapproval and rejection are similar, they are certainly not synonymous. Disapproval occurs when someone shows you that he or she dislikes you or some aspect of you, but has not rejected you, meaning you have not been expelled from that person's life. Rejection, on the other hand, occurs when you are expelled from someone's life. Most often this occurs because the person doesn't like you, but not necessarily. Thus, one of my clients only wanted casual relationships with men at this stage of her life. She then met a man she got on very well with and thought that there was a good chance that if she went out with him she would fall in love with him. As a result, she rejected him in the sense that she told him she did not want to see him again because he posed a threat to her.

In this chapter I will discuss both disapproval-based situations and rejection-based situations, sometimes separately and at other times together.

Dealing with disapproval and rejection *per se*

When you disturb yourself about being disapproved or rejected and this is the only thing that you are in fact disturbing yourself about, then your disturbance will concern either your sense of self-esteem or the discomfort that is inherent with disapproval or rejection.

To illustrate the above point, I will discuss the cases of Robin and Richard, who were rejected on the same day by different women in identical circumstances.

The case of Robin: self-esteem disturbance

Robin had been going out with his girlfriend for about a year. After he returned from holiday, his girlfriend told him that she no longer wanted to see him because while he was away she had met someone else, had fallen in love with him and wanted to pursue a relationship with him. Robin was depressed about this rejection. Let's see why. In working with Robin in counselling, his CBT therapist helped him to formulate the following ABC:

A = *My girlfriend rejected me.*
B = *'I absolutely should not have been rejected by my girlfriend and the fact that I have been proves that I am unlovable.'*
C (emotional) = *Depression.*
    (behavioural) = *Ongoing withdrawal and refusal to meet other women.*
    (thinking) = *'No other woman will ever love me.'*

How Robin overcame the challenge of being rejected and moved on

Robin questioned and changed his irrational belief and developed an alternative rational belief. This led him to experience a healthier negative emotion, and his subsequent behaviour and thinking encouraged him to move on with his life after a period of mourning his loss. What follows is Robin's new ABC, which summarizes the changes that he made.

A = *My girlfriend rejected me.*
B = *'I wish my girlfriend had not rejected me, but sadly there is no reason I absolutely should not have been rejected by her. The fact that she did reject me does not prove that I am unlovable. I am a fallible human being who is capable of being loved and not being loved by women.'*

C (emotional) = *Sadness.*

(behavioural) = *Mourning the loss and then going out to meet new women.*

(thinking) = *'There will be women who will love me. I just have to find one whom I will also love.'*

The case of Richard: discomfort disturbance

Like Robin, Richard had been going out with his girlfriend for about a year. After he returned from holiday, his girlfriend also told him that she no longer wanted to go out with him because while he was away she had met someone else, had fallen in love with him and wanted to pursue a relationship with him. Like Robin, Richard was also depressed about this rejection. Again, let's see why. In working with Richard in counselling, his CBT therapist helped him to formulate the following ABC.

A = *My girlfriend rejected me.*

B = *'I absolutely should not have been rejected by my girlfriend and I can't stand the discomfort of being rejected.'*

C (emotional) = *Agitated anxiety.*

(behavioural) = *Drinking alcohol and going out to bars to meet women.*

(thinking) = *'I need to find another woman quickly to forget about being rejected.'*

How Richard overcame the challenge of being rejected and moved on

Richard also questioned and changed his irrational belief and developed an alternative rational belief. This led him to experience a healthier negative emotion, and his subsequent behaviour and thinking also encouraged him to move on with his life. What follows is Richard's new ABC, which summarizes the changes that he made.

A = *My girlfriend rejected me.*

B = *'I wish my girlfriend had not rejected me, but I do not have to be immune from such rejection and nor was I, as it turned out! I can stand the discomfort of being rejected, even though it is painful. It is worth tolerating because I do want to get on with my life.'*

C (emotional) = *Concern.*

(behavioural) = *Refraining from drinking to excess and from going out in a desperate way to meet another woman. Instead,*

going out with my friends and drinking sensibly. Talking about my feelings rather than drinking them away.
(thinking) = *'I don't need to find another woman quickly to forget about being rejected. I need to come to terms with the discomfort of being rejected before dating again.'*

You will see that while Robin and Richard held the same rigid belief (i.e. 'I absolutely should not have been rejected by my girlfriend') they held different extreme beliefs about rejection. Robin's extreme belief centred on his unlovability (which is an example of what we call 'ego disturbance' in CBT, where the person depreciates him- or herself in some way). By contrast, Richard's extreme belief centred on his perceived inability to tolerate the discomfort of being rejected (which is an example of discomfort disturbance). These examples show that while rigid demands give rise to disturbance, on their own they do not indicate what kind of disturbance the person will experience. We need to know the person's extreme beliefs for that.

The same point can also be made about Robin and Richard's flexible beliefs. While they give rise to a psychologically healthy response, on their own they do not indicate what kind of healthy response the person will make. We need to know the person's non-extreme beliefs for that. Robin's non-extreme belief centred on his self-acceptance, while Richard's non-extreme belief centred on his perceived ability to tolerate the discomfort of being rejected (which is an example of discomfort tolerance).

Dealing with disapproval or rejection when it means that you won't be looked after

Malcolm

Malcolm had just been rejected by his girlfriend. He was terribly depressed and had to be hospitalized, and was referred to me after he was discharged. Malcolm was a 32-year-old man who had always been dependent on women. He lived at home with his parents, and his mother did virtually everything for him. He was quite happy with this and had dated a number of women, but nothing serious until he met Melanie. Malcolm and Melanie became quite close very quickly and after a great deal of soul-searching Malcolm decided to take up Melanie's offer for him to move in with her. When he did, it was a very different experience from the one Melanie was hoping for.

When they were dating, Malcolm was quite assertive and manly, comfortable in the knowledge that his mother was in the background and that he could always rely on her emotionally. After he moved in with Melanie, Malcolm's mother had a stroke and had to be looked after by Malcolm's father. Malcolm reacted to this news by being very dependent on Melanie. He looked to her to supply the same level of emotional support that his mother had always supplied him.

Melanie, on the other hand, was hoping that she could continue to look up to this assertive and very masculine man and was shocked to see the transformation in Malcolm after his mother's stroke. The last thing Melanie wanted was a man who was emotionally dependent on her, but that is exactly what she got. Rather than attempting to work things through with Malcolm, she ended the relationship and told Malcolm to leave. Malcolm reacted to this rejection by collapsing emotionally. He became very depressed and agitated and, as I said earlier, had to be admitted to hospital, unable to be left alone as he was threatening to commit suicide.

Malcolm had collapsed because for him rejection meant that he had nobody to look after him. He held the irrational belief very strongly that he needed a woman to look after him emotionally, and for the first time in his life he did not have one as his mother was in no state to offer him the emotional support he was used to.

Malcolm's ABC

Let me put the salient points of Malcolm's story into ABC form:

A = *Melanie's rejection of me means that I have no woman in my life to look after me emotionally.*

B = *'I absolutely need a woman to look after me emotionally and I can't tolerate it when this condition is absent from my life.'*

C (emotional) = *Depressed and suicidal.*
(behavioural) = *Severe withdrawal into self; agitated pacing; seeking a woman to look after me.*
(thinking) = *'I cannot care for myself emotionally. My life is over unless I find another woman to look after me and find one quickly.'*

Malcolm was in counselling for almost a year, in which time he questioned his irrational belief and developed a rational alternative. The main thrust of counselling was on helping Malcolm to see that he could care for himself emotionally if he allowed himself to.

As Malcolm's depression lifted, he began to look around for another woman to look after him and found one who was co-dependent (meaning that she needed being needed), which from a long-term psychological perspective was the last thing Malcolm needed. I was not surprised at this development, since being emotionally reliant on a female was a familiar state for Malcolm and when humans are uncomfortable they naturally turn to the familiar to restore a sense of comfort. I helped Malcolm to understand the reason behind him starting this relationship, and to his credit he ended it immediately.

Therapy had two phases with Malcolm. For the first six months he decided not to go out with women. Rather, he focused on developing self-caring and self-soothing skills that were not in his repertoire. In the past, as soon as he needed emotional support or soothing he turned to his mother, who gave it readily. Malcolm began to keep a diary in which he learned to talk to himself in an emotionally self-supportive way through journal entries. Therapy was another way in which he learned to support himself. In my view it was important that I am male, since if Malcolm had had a female therapist he might have replicated the situation where a woman (in this case a female therapist) gave him emotional support, and this might have delayed the development of his self-support.

The second phase of therapy with Malcolm began when he began a new relationship with a woman called Angela. I encouraged Malcolm to list all the ways he might rely on Angela emotionally, and for every way we developed an alternative whereby Malcolm supported himself instead. He began to have the novel experience of being emotionally self-supportive while in a relationship with a woman, and later began to learn how to have a relationship which was mutually supportive. Here, just because Malcolm allowed Angela to support him emotionally at times did not mean that he could stop being emotionally self-supportive. Managing this new state of affairs was difficult for Malcolm at first, as you might expect, but he gradually learned the true value of being in a mutually supportive relationship where both partners retained a sense of individuality as well as being together.

Malcolm's new ABC

Let me now provide Malcolm's new ABC when later, sadly, he was rejected by Angela (but not because he was clingy):

> A = *Angela's rejection of me means that I have no woman in my life to look after me emotionally.*

B = 'I don't need a woman to look after me emotionally, even though it is nice to have the emotional support that comes from being in a relationship. I can definitely tolerate it when this condition is absent from my life and can continue to provide it for myself, as I have learned to do over the past year.'

C (emotional) = *Sadness.*

(behavioural) = *Mourning the loss and staying connected to my circle of friends. Not seeking a new woman until I feel ready.*

(thinking) = *'I can care for myself emotionally. My life is less rich at the moment, but it won't be enriched by another woman until I am ready to find one. There is much more to my life than having a woman to share it with.'*

General guidelines for dealing with disapproval and rejection when it means that you won't be looked after

When you have been rejected and you disturb yourself about not being looked after, I suggest you do the following:

1 Identify your demand that you must be looked after and your extreme belief, normally that you can't bear not to be looked after.

2 Challenge these beliefs and develop their rational alternatives ('I prefer to be looked after, but I don't need to be. I can bear not to be looked after although it is a struggle').

3 Identify your self-view that makes you vulnerable to the rejection-based loss of a caretaker (e.g. 'I am too weak to support myself').

4 Do a cost–benefit analysis of this self-view and its less vulnerable alternative (e.g. 'I may struggle, but I am strong enough to support myself').

5 If your cost–benefit analysis reveals that it is in your interests to develop your stronger self-view, implement points 6–9 below.

6 Make a list of all the things that you rely on other people for, and develop alternative self-reliant behaviours that you can do instead.

7 Resolve to act in a self-reliant, self-supportive manner, even when you experience the urge to rely on others.

8 When you go back to your old other-reliant ways, accept yourself for doing so and learn from the experience.

9 Keep practising your self-reliant, self-supportive behaviours. Your self-view will change, but only when you have put in the healthy practice.

Dealing with disapproval or rejection when it means loss of advantages

Some people disturb themselves when they are disapproved not because they care that much about having the other person's approval *per se*, but because they think that if they lose the approval of the other, then they will lose the advantages that go (or are judged to go) with such approval.

For example, Gina was very friendly with her supervisor at work. The supervisor was very kind to her and, as Gina saw it, gave her all kinds of advantages (e.g. the best shifts and time off for non-urgent medical and dental appointments). However, her supervisor considered that Gina had started taking advantage of her by turning up late for work. As a result, the supervisor rebuked Gina and became less friendly towards her. Gina disturbed herself about her supervisor's disapproval, not because she cared very much about what the supervisor thought of her as a person, but because she thought that she would lose the advantages she had gained by having a good relationship with the supervisor.

Here is Gina's ABC:

A = *My supervisor's disapproval means that I will lose the advantages that she has given me.*

B = *'I must not lose the advantages and it would be terrible if I did.'*

C (emotional) = *Anxiety.*
(behavioural) = *Being extra nice to my supervisor to regain her approval so I can get back the advantages.*
(thinking) = *'Losing the advantages will mean that my job will be bleak.'*

So what will Gina have to do to effectively address her disturbance about the lost advantages, assuming that she does lose them? Her new ABC below makes this clear.

A = *My supervisor's disapproval means that I will lose the advantages that she has given me.*

B = *'I would prefer not to lose the advantages, but there is no law to say that I must not lose them. It would be bad to lose them, but not terrible.'*

C (emotional) = *Concern.*
(behavioural) = *Doing my job well and learning from my mistake of taking my supervisor for granted.*

(thinking) = *'Losing the advantages will mean that my job will be harder rather than bleak.'*

General guidelines for dealing with disapproval and rejection when it means loss of advantages

Here are some general guidelines that you can follow for dealing healthily with the loss of advantages that stems from disapproval and rejection.

1 Assume that you will lose the advantages as the result of the disapproval or rejection.
2 Identify the irrational beliefs about the loss of the advantages, particularly your rigid demand and LFT belief.
3 Challenge these beliefs and develop rational beliefs, particularly your flexible and HFT beliefs.
4 Make the most of your situation despite losing the advantages.
5 Reflect on the place of these advantages and what you are prepared to do to get them in the future.

Dealing with when you overestimate disapproval and rejection and attempt to prevent them from happening

So far in this chapter, I have dealt with situations where you have been disapproved or rejected. However, you may act to prevent disapproval and rejection from happening because you think that they are imminent, even when there is no clear-cut evidence that they are about to happen.

Why might you think that disapproval and rejection are imminent in the absence of such clear-cut evidence? Because you hold a general irrational belief that links the need to be approved and accepted with the need for certainty that you are approved and accepted. It works like this. When you enter a situation where you believe that you need to be approved and accepted and it is not clear that you will be, your need for certainty means that if you cannot convince yourself that you will be approved and accepted then you conclude that you will be disapproved and rejected (see Chapter 4 for a discussion of the need for certainty and its effects).

Since you think that disapproval and rejection are imminent and you would disturb yourself if they did happen, you then do your best to make sure that they do not happen.

People who overestimate disapproval and rejection, for reasons that I have discussed above, generally use two major strategies: (1) being more than usually nice to people to 'pull' an approving or accepting response from them; (2) refraining from asserting themselves in case it provokes disapproval or rejection from others.

Brenda sought CBT because she was often used and manipulated by others. She was always very nice to people and very accommodating to them, often offering to do favours for them. While she resented it when people took advantage of her good nature, she was too scared to do anything about it.

When I assessed Brenda's problems, I discovered the following.

1 She had the following general irrational belief concerning disapproval and rejection: 'I must be approved and accepted by people and if I am not I am worthless.'

2 She had the following general irrational belief about uncertainty related to approval and acceptance: 'I must know for certain that people who matter to me approve and accept me and I can't bear not knowing whether they do or not.' This irrational belief led her to think that uncertainty meant that if she did not do anything to get them to approve of her, then these people would disapprove of her. In this way Brenda overestimated the extent to which people would disapprove and reject her.

3 Whenever Brenda was in a state of uncertainty about disapproval and rejection, she acted in a way that was designed to get people to approve and accept her. Consequently, she never tested her inference that uncertainty would lead to disapproval and rejection if she did not do something to prevent this from happening.

4 Whenever people took advantage of her she did nothing about it for fear that they might disapprove or reject her.

With my help, Brenda did the following:

1 She challenged her general irrational belief about disapproval and rejection and developed the following general rational belief instead: 'I would like to be approved and accepted by people, but it is not necessary for them to do so. If I am not accepted and approved that is bad, but I am not worthless. I can accept myself in the face of disapproval and rejection.'

2 She challenged her general irrational belief about uncertainty related to approval and acceptance and developed the following general rational belief: 'I would like to know for certain that people who matter to me approve and accept me, but I don't have to know this.

I can bear not having such certainty and it's worth it for me to do so.' This rational belief led her to think that uncertainty meant just that: uncertainty. In this way, Brenda began to see that it was probable that people would approve and accept her when she was in a state of uncertainty.

3 Whenever Brenda was in a state of uncertainty about disapproval and rejection, she did not do anything designed to get people to approve and accept her. In this way, she tested her inference that uncertainty would lead to disapproval and rejection without trying to prevent them from occurring. She found that, by and large, people still approved and accepted her under these conditions, and when they didn't she used the appropriate rational belief to deal with this.

4 Whenever people took advantage of her she began to assert herself and practised her new developing rational belief about disapproval and rejection at the same time. As a result, people began to respect her limits and stopped taking advantage of her. Only one or two people rejected her and she coped well with these rejections by practising her new rational belief.

General guidelines for dealing with overestimating disapproval and rejection and attempting to prevent them from happening

Here are some general guidelines that you can follow for dealing healthily with when you overestimate disapproval and rejection and when you attempt to prevent them from happening.

1 Identify and challenge your general irrational belief about disapproval and rejection and develop an alternative general rational belief instead.

2 Identify and challenge your general irrational belief about uncertainty as it relates to disapproval and rejection and develop an alternative general rational belief instead.

3 Show yourself that when you are uncertain about whether people approve and accept you or not, then it is probable that they do not disapprove or will reject you, unless you have clear evidence to the contrary. Do not do anything that is designed to prevent these people from disapproving or rejecting you, so that you can test out what actually happens when you are in this state of uncertainty.

4 Assert yourself when people misuse or take advantage of you and practise your rational belief about disapproval and rejection as you

do so. See how they actually respond to your assertion in the short and longer term.

In the next and final chapter of this book, I will discuss how you can deal effectively with unfairness, injustice and betrayal.

8

Dealing with unfairness, injustice and betrayal

Introduction

In this final chapter, I will deal with an adversity that many find very difficult to move on from. Indeed, many never really do, and allow themselves to be haunted by unfairness, injustice or betrayal for their entire lives.

You may think that unfairness, injustice and betrayal are synonymous, but there are differences among them.

In my view, unfairness describes a situation where you may fail to get a reward that someone else gets or you may get a penalty that someone else escapes. In the first situation, you think that you deserve to get the reward, and in the second, you think that you did not deserve to get the penalty. As I am using the term, unfairness involves a comparison between you and someone else, where you think that you have fared badly through no fault of your own.

Injustice occurs when your expectation of receiving legal or quasi-legal justice is not met. Indeed, you may even get the opposite of what you expect.

Finally, betrayal is far more personal, in my view. It occurs when you trust someone and think that there is no chance that your trust will be betrayed, but it is.

I will deal with each of these in turn, showing you how you may disturb yourself about these challenges and how you can deal with this disturbance and thence move on with your life. I will also discuss common obstacles that may prevent you from moving on, and will suggest ways of addressing these obstacles, should you wish to address them.

Dealing with unfairness-related disturbance

In order to deal with your disturbance about unfairness, you first need to understand the factors involved in your disturbance. When you disturb yourself about unfairness, the following elements seem to be present.

You make an interpretation of unfairness

First, something happens that you interpret as being unfair to you (or to a significant other or others). Two scenarios are common here.

- Scenario 1: Undeserved failure to get something positive.
  - Someone gets something positive that you do not get.
  - You think that you deserved to get it instead of or as well as the other person.
  - You may think that the other person did not deserve to get it.
- Scenario 2: Undeserved receipt of something negative.
  - You get something negative that someone else does not get.
  - You think that you did not deserve to get it.
  - You may think that the other person deserved to get it.

In the ABC framework of CBT that I discussed in Chapter 1, your interpretation of unfairness is made at 'A' in that framework. The important point to remember here is that when you disturb yourself, you think that your interpretation of unfairness is true whether or not the facts support your interpretation. Indeed, you will find that when you disturb yourself about the unfairness that you experienced, you will not listen to attempts by people to convince you that what you experienced was not unfair. Consequently, in order to discover how you disturbed yourself about the unfairness and thence to help you deal with your disturbance, we encourage you in CBT to assume temporarily that your interpretation was correct and that you were treated unfairly. The best time to question this is when you have dealt with your unfairness-based disturbance.

You hold a set of irrational beliefs about the unfairness

Consistent with the position that I have taken throughout this book, when you disturb yourself about unfairness you hold a set of irrational beliefs about this unfairness. It is important that you recognize, therefore, that unfairness, on its own, does not make you disturbed. Rather, it contributes to your disturbance by triggering your irrational beliefs. As we will see, blaming your disturbance on the unfairness *per se* is a major obstacle to dealing effectively with it.

Rigid demand

At the heart of your disturbance about unfairness is a rigid demand. Here, you are not just saying that it would have been much better for you if the unfairness had not happened: you are rigidly demanding that it absolutely should not have happened. When pressed for a reason, you would probably say that it should not have happened because you did not deserve it. This reveals an important point about unfairness-related disturbance. It is often based on the following demands, which I will relate to the two scenarios described above:

- Scenario 1: I must get the fairness that I deserve.
- Scenario 2: I must not get the unfairness that I do not deserve.

Extreme beliefs

While a few people will disturb themselves about undeserved unfairness by switching focus, concluding that they did deserve to be treated unfairly after all and then depreciating themselves as a result, I will not discuss this rarer form of unfairness-related disturbance here. Rather, I will focus on the more common forms of unfairness-related disturbance, in which you hold the following extreme beliefs, all of which stem from rigid demands.

- *Awfulizing beliefs* Here, you don't just say that it is bad that you were treated unfairly: you hold that it is terrible, awful or the end of the world that this happened.
- *LFT beliefs* Here you don't just say that it is difficult to put up with the unfairness: you hold that it is unbearable.
- *Depreciation beliefs* Here, I will discuss other-depreciation beliefs and life-depreciation beliefs. In the former, if you judge that somebody is responsible for the unfairness that happened to you, you not only think that what was done was bad, you also hold that the person is bad for doing this. In the latter, you don't just say that the unfairness was bad, you also hold that life is bad for allowing this unfairness to occur.

You experience a number of disturbed responses when you hold a set of irrational beliefs about the unfairness

When you hold a set of irrational beliefs, you experience a variety of emotional, behavioural and thinking effects. Most of these effects are evidence of psychological disturbance and will stop you from moving on from the unfairness.

Here is a partial list of these effects:

- *Emotions* Depression; unhealthy anger (including long-term resentment and bitterness); hurt; and self-pity.
- *Behaviours* Withdrawal from life; aggression (including getting revenge and carrying out vendettas); sulking; and constant complaining.
- *Thinking* Hopelessness; predicting future unfairness; plotting revenge; focusing on past unfairness; editing out past fairness and the prospect of future fairness.

How to respond to your unfairness-related disturbance

Here is how to respond to your unfairness-related disturbance.

Assume that your interpretation of unfairness is true

As I pointed out earlier in this section, it is important that, in order to deal with your disturbance about unfairness, you assume temporarily that your interpretation of unfairness is true.

Challenge your set of irrational beliefs about the unfairness and develop an alternative rational set

In challenging your irrational beliefs about unfairness and developing alternative rational beliefs, you need to show yourself a number of things which in my view are equivalent to swallowing a bitter pill. It will do you good, but may be hard to digest.

Challenge your rigid demand and develop a flexible belief You need to show yourself that, sadly and regrettably, there is no law of the universe to decree that the unfairness that you are facing absolutely should not have occurred. If such a law existed, the unfairness would not have happened to you because it could not have happened to you. The grim reality is that it did happen to you, and if you cling to your demand you will have two types of unfairness for the price of one: the unfairness that happened to you and the unfairness of self-disturbance about the original unfairness.

Let me apply these flexible beliefs to the two scenarios that I listed earlier in this chapter (see page 100).

- Scenario 1: Just because I deserve to be treated fairly does not mean that I have to be so. It would be nice, but what is nice does not have to exist.
- Scenario 2: Just because I don't deserve to be treated unfairly does

not mean that this must not happen to me. Again, it would be nice, but it does not have to be the way I want it to be.

Challenge your extreme beliefs and develop non-extreme beliefs

Non-awfulizing beliefs instead of awfulizing beliefs Here, you need to show yourself that however bad the unfairness is, it is not true that it was terrible, awful or the end of the world that this happened. If it were true, then no good could possibly come of it and good things in the future could not possibly happen to you. Remember what Smokey Robinson's mother said: 'Son, from the day you are born till you ride in the hearse, there's nothing so bad that it couldn't be worse.' This is not designed to minimize the badness of the unfairness, but to take the horror out of the unfairness.

HFT beliefs instead of LFT beliefs Here, you need to show yourself that while you may 'feel' that you cannot bear the unfairness, having this 'feeling' doesn't prove that you can't put up with it. You would do so to save the life of a loved one and you can do so for yourself as well, if you show yourself that it is worth it to you to do so. Why is it worth it? The reason is that doing so will help you to move on with your life. Not that this means that you will forget that the unfairness happened. You won't. But it will mean that it won't dominate and ruin your life, unless you let it by clinging to your LFT belief.

Acceptance beliefs instead of depreciation beliefs If you hold an other-depreciation belief, you need to show yourself that if another person was responsible for perpetrating the unfairness against you, then that action was bad but it does not mean that the person is bad for acting badly. The person's identity is not determined by these actions and, in fact, he or she is a fallible human being capable of acting well and badly and not just capable of acting badly. This does not mean that you have to forget what was done, but it will help you to forgive the person and move on.

If you hold a life-depreciation belief, you need to show yourself that while the unfairness was bad it does not follow that life is all bad for allowing this unfairness to occur. Life, in truth, is a complex mixture of the good, the bad and the neutral. Reminding yourself of this will help you to move forward and live in this complex world.

You will experience a number of constructive and healthy responses if you develop the above set of rational beliefs

When you develop a set of rational beliefs about the unfairness, and you act and think in ways that are consistent with them, eventually these ways of behaving and thinking will take root and your feelings will begin to change. A partial list of these new consequences of your developing rational beliefs is shown below:

- *Emotions* Sadness (as opposed to depression); healthy anger (as opposed to unhealthy anger); sorrow and disappointment (as opposed to hurt and self-pity).
- *Behaviours* Staying connected with life (as opposed to withdrawing from it); assertion (as opposed to aggression and sulking); and refraining from talking about the unfairness to others (as opposed to constant complaining).
- *Thinking* Viewing the future realistically (as opposed to viewing it with hopelessness); predicting future fairness and unfairness (as opposed to just predicting unfairness); thinking about how to assert yourself (as opposed to plotting revenge); focusing on past fairness and unfairness (as opposed to focusing just on past unfairness); reminding yourself about past fairness and the prospect of future fairness (as opposed to editing out both of these).

Obstacles to dealing with unfairness-based disturbance and how to address them

As I mentioned at the beginning of this chapter, some people experience a number of obstacles in utilizing the CBT approach in dealing with their disturbance about unfairness, injustice and betrayal. In this section, I will briefly list the three main obstacles to dealing with unfairness-related disturbance and show how you can address these obstacles.

Obstacle 1

'If I give up my demand about the unfairness happening, I am condoning the unfairness.'

Response: 'I can give up the demand without condoning the unfairness. The one does not follow from the other. In fact, they are not connected unless I connect them.'

Obstacle 2

'If I give up my extreme awfulizing belief about the unfairness, I am minimizing the badness of it.'

Response: 'When I take the horror out of something that is very bad, like the unfairness, I am still left with the view that it was very bad. So, a non-awfulizing belief is not designed to minimize badness. It is designed to eliminate horror.'

Obstacle 3

'If I accept that the person who was responsible for the unfairness is fallible, rather than bad, then I am letting him or her off the hook.'

Response: 'I can accept the other person as fallible and still hold that person responsible for his or her actions.'

How Jacob dealt with his unfairness-related disturbance

Jacob and his work colleague were both promised promotion at work by their manager, but only his colleague got it. Jacob was given no reason why he wasn't promoted. He first reacted to this unfairness with unhealthy anger, because he demanded that he absolutely should not have been treated so unfairly, and he was tempted to put a number of viruses into the company's computer network. This served as a wake-up call for him and he challenged his rigid demand about the unfairness and developed a flexible belief instead (i.e. 'I wish I wasn't treated unfairly, but that does not mean it absolutely should not have happened to me'). Consequently, he experienced healthy anger and wrote an assertive letter of complaint to the managing director, which resulted in him receiving his promotion.

Injustice-related disturbance

Dealing with injustice-related disturbance is similar to dealing with unfairness-related disturbance. As such, I will not repeat myself and while noting the similarities as we proceed, I will focus particularly on the differences. I suggest that you refer back to the appropriate material in the section on 'Unfairness-related disturbance' where necessary.

In order to deal with your disturbance about injustice, you first need to understand the factors involved in your disturbance. When you disturb yourself about injustice the following elements will be present.

You make an interpretation of injustice

As I said earlier in this chapter, injustice occurs within a more formal legal or quasi-legal context, where you have been treated (or think you have been treated) in a way that is inconsistent with justice, as defined in that context. Injustice also includes a sense that you have done nothing to deserve the injustice that has happened to you.

You hold a set of irrational beliefs about the injustice

In the ABC framework of CBT that I discussed in Chapter 1, your interpretation that you have been treated unjustly occurs at 'A' and, however difficult this is to accept, the injustice, on its own, did not cause your disturbance. Rather, your disturbance is based on the irrational beliefs that you held about the injustice.

Rigid demand

At the heart of your disturbance about injustice is a rigid demand. Here, you are not just saying that it would have been much better for you if the injustice had not happened: you are rigidly demanding that it absolutely should not have happened. When pressed for a reason why it should not have happened, you would probably say because you felt it was unjust. Thus, you believe that when something can be proved to be unjust, it absolutely should not happen to you. You also believe that you have to fight and achieve justice in the end.

Extreme beliefs

Here, I will focus on disturbance where the person is not depreciating him- or herself for being treated unjustly. As I outline the following extreme beliefs, bear in mind that in CBT they are deemed to stem from rigid demands.

- *Awfulizing beliefs* Here, you don't just say that it is bad that you were treated unjustly, you hold that it is terrible, awful or the end of the world that this happened. You also hold that it will be terrible, awful and the end of the world if you cannot get justice in the end.
- *LFT beliefs* Here you don't just say that it is difficult to put up with the injustice, you hold that it is unbearable, as is the idea that justice cannot be achieved in the end.
- *Depreciation beliefs* Here, I will discuss other-depreciation beliefs and life depreciation beliefs. In the former, if you think that somebody is responsible for the injustice that happened to you, then you believe that the person is bad for doing so. You also think this way if you consider that someone stands in the way of you getting justice. In the latter, you don't just say that the injustice was bad, you hold that life is bad for allowing it to occur and also for not allowing justice to be eventually achieved.

You experience a number of disturbed responses when you hold a set of irrational beliefs about the injustice

When you hold a set of irrational beliefs, you experience a variety of emotional, behavioural and thinking effects. Most of these effects are evidence of psychological disturbance and will stop you from moving on from the unfairness. They also occur at different times in the process.

Initially, you will experience a sense of disbelief, followed by unhealthy anger when it has dawned on you that an injustice has happened to you. This unhealthy anger will drive you to put all your energy into righting the wrong that has befallen you, but in an obsessive, all-consuming way. You will be preoccupied by thoughts about the injustice and how you can get justice.

If you reach the stage where you acknowledge that justice cannot be achieved, your irrational beliefs about this will lead you to become depressed and withdraw from life, losing interest in your case and, indeed, in everything else. 'He was a broken man' is a phrase often used to describe a person (male in this case) in this situation.

How to respond to your injustice-related disturbance

Here is how to respond to your injustice-related disturbance.

Assume that your interpretation of injustice is true

If you don't do this you won't be able to move easily to the next point as you will get caught up in a debate about what is just and what is unjust.

Challenge your set of irrational beliefs about the injustice and develop an alternative rational set

In challenging your irrational beliefs about injustice and developing helpful alternative rational beliefs, you need to show yourself a number of things which you may find unpalatable.

Challenge your rigid demand and develop a flexible belief You need to show yourself that, sadly and regrettably, there is no law of the universe to decree that the injustice you are facing absolutely should not have occurred, nor that justice has to triumph in the end. Both these things would be highly desirable for you, but sadly, as you don't run the universe, you cannot guarantee their existence.

Challenge your extreme beliefs and develop non-extreme beliefs

Non-awfulizing beliefs instead of awfulizing beliefs Here, you need to show yourself that, however bad the injustice, it is not true that it is terrible, awful or the end of the world that this happened. Nor is it terrible, awful or the end of the world if justice does not triumph in the end. This would also be very bad, but you can move on from it if you take the horror out of it.

HFT beliefs instead of LFT beliefs Here, you need to show yourself that while you may think that you cannot bear the injustice happening in the first place or justice not finally triumphing in the second place, you can put up with both, albeit with difficulty. Is it worth it to you to do so? The answer to this question is 'yes' if you want to move on with your life, and 'no' if you don't!

Acceptance beliefs instead of depreciation beliefs When you hold an other-depreciation belief, you need to show yourself that if another person was responsible for perpetrating the injustice against you or for preventing justice from occurring, then again such actions are bad, but that does not mean that the people involved are bad humans. Such people are not thoroughly bad for acting badly, even though you may 'feel' that they are. Your 'feeling' is only evidence that your belief is irrational and not that it is true. In reality, the people concerned are fallible human beings and you need to work towards accepting this fact if you want to move on with your life.

If you hold a life-depreciation belief, you need to show yourself that while the injustice was bad, life is not all bad for allowing this unfairness to occur in the first place and for not giving you justice in the final analysis. Life is not a Hollywood movie where justice triumphs in the end and, in truth, it is a complex mixture of the just and the unjust. Reminding yourself of this will help you to move forward and live in this complex world.

You will experience a number of constructive responses if you develop the above set of rational beliefs

When you develop a set of rational beliefs about the injustice, and you act and think in ways that are consistent with them, eventually these ways of behaving and thinking will take root and your feelings will begin to change.

While you will still experience an initial sense of disbelief that the injustice could happen to you, if you think rationally about the injustice you will feel healthy anger (as opposed to unhealthy anger) when it has dawned on you what has happened to you. This healthy anger will lead you to work towards righting the wrong that has befallen you, but not in an obsessive, all-consuming way and not to the exclusion of the other responsibilities in your life. You will still have thoughts about the injustice and how you can get justice, but not in a preoccupied manner.

If you reach the stage where you acknowledge that the justice cannot be achieved, your rational beliefs about this will lead you to become sad but not depressed about it. You will move on with life and not withdraw from it. In short, you will be a wiser man or woman, but not 'broken'.

Obstacles to dealing with injustice-based disturbance and how to address them

In this section, I will briefly list the three main obstacles to dealing with injustice-related disturbance and show how you can address them.

Obstacle 1

'If I give up my demand about righting the wrong, I will give up trying to right the wrong.'

Response: 'If I give up the demand, I am attempting to give up my disturbance. I can still try to right the wrong as long as the wrong can be put right.'

Obstacle 2

'If I give up trying to right the wrong, I am legitimizing the injustice.'

Response: 'If it appears that I cannot right the wrong, it will make sense to give up trying to do so. Doing this does not mean that I am legitimizing the injustice, even if some people may think so. Giving up means that I am no longer trying to change what cannot be changed.'

Obstacle 3

'If I show myself that I can tolerate the injustice, I am showing that I don't care that it happened to me.'

Response: 'I can tolerate the injustice as a way of undisturbing myself about it. Lack of disturbance does not mean I don't care. I can care very much, with or without disturbance.'

How Harry did not deal with his injustice-related disturbance

Unfortunately, not every story has a happy ending and this sadly applies in Harry's case. Harry saw a motorist speaking on her mobile phone at a zebra crossing and asked her to stop. When she refused he blocked her path and called the police. When the police arrived they let the motorist go, since they said there was no concrete or corroborative evidence of an offence – in fact, they charged Harry instead, for causing an obstruction in the road. He was taken to court and given a fine and a warning as to his future behaviour. Harry was incensed because he held the following belief: 'Because I was only being a good citizen, I absolutely should not have been prosecuted, as this was unjust, and this injustice must not be allowed to stand.' Harry became consumed with righting this wrong and became obsessed with clearing his name, writing hundreds of letters and spending thousands of pounds on legal bills. After two years he gave up, became depressed and suicidal and refused all offers of psychological help. He resisted such help because, in his mind, accepting it would mean that he was the one with the problem, and not British justice. He retired early on ill-health grounds, a 'broken man'.

Dealing with betrayal-related disturbance

Once again, dealing with betrayal-related disturbance is similar to dealing with unfairness-related disturbance. There are differences and I will concentrate on these in the material that follows, while noting the similarities as we proceed. Once again, I suggest that you consult the appropriate material in the section on 'Unfairness-related disturbance' (pages 98–104) if you need to.

In order to deal with your disturbance about being betrayed, you first need to understand the factors involved in your disturbance. When you disturb yourself about being betrayed the following elements are present.

You make an interpretation that you have been betrayed

First, somebody close to you has done something or failed to do something that you interpret as a betrayal. Given your relationship with the person, you would not have dreamed that he or she would have acted (or failed to act) in this way. Here, 'betrayal' is shorthand for a betrayal of your trust.

You hold a set of irrational beliefs about the betrayal

Consistent with the position that I have taken throughout this book, when you disturb yourself about being betrayed, you hold a set of irrational beliefs about this betrayal. It is these beliefs rather than the betrayal itself that account for your disturbed responses. This may be difficult for you to accept, but is true nonetheless.

Rigid demand

At the heart of your disturbance about being betrayed is a rigid demand. Here, you are not just saying that it would have been much better for you if the person had not betrayed your trust: you are rigidly demanding that he or she absolutely should not have done so. When pressed for a reason why this should not have happened, you would probably say it was because you trusted him or her. This reveals an important point about betrayal-related disturbance. It is often based on the idea that because you trusted the person, he or she absolutely should not have betrayed your trust.

Extreme beliefs

In this section, I will focus on the most common form of betrayal-related disturbance, in which you hold the following extreme beliefs, all of which stem from rigid demands.

- *Awfulizing beliefs* Here you don't just say that it is bad that you were betrayed, you hold that it is terrible, awful or the end of the world that this happened.
- *LFT beliefs* Here, you don't just say that it is difficult to put up with being betrayed, you hold that it is unbearable and that you are a poor person for being treated in such a way.
- *Depreciation beliefs* Here, I will discuss other-depreciation beliefs and life-depreciation beliefs. In the former, you think that the person who betrayed you is bad for acting badly towards you. In the latter, you don't just say that the betrayal was bad, you hold that life is bad for allowing this person to betray you in the way that he or she did.

You experience a number of disturbed responses when you hold a set of irrational beliefs about the betrayal

Your main emotional responses are hurt, unhealthy anger and depression. You tend to withdraw from life and sulk, and suppress your urge to hurt the person in the way that you think he or she has hurt you. You tend to think that men (or women) are not to be trusted and that you will never risk being betrayed again.

How to respond to your betrayal-related disturbance

Here is how to respond to your betrayal-related disturbance.

Assume that your interpretation of betrayal is true

I have argued several times that the reason it is best to assume temporarily that 'A' (in this case, betrayal) is true is because it helps you to identify the irrational beliefs that are at the root of your disturbance (in this case, about being betrayed).

Challenge your set of irrational beliefs about the betrayal and develop an alternative rational set

In challenging your irrational beliefs about betrayal and developing alternative rational beliefs, you need to show yourself a number of things which are again hard to take.

Challenge your rigid demand and develop a flexible belief

You need to show yourself that, sadly and regrettably, there is no law of the universe to decree that just because you trusted someone, he or she absolutely should not have betrayed that trust. If such a law existed this could not have happened because the law of the universe would have stopped him or her. The grim reality is that the person did betray your trust.

Challenge your extreme beliefs and develop non-extreme beliefs

Non-awfulizing beliefs instead of awfulizing beliefs Here, you need to show yourself that however bad the betrayal was, it is not true that it was terrible, awful or the end of the world that this happened. You can learn from the experience and consider the possibility that your assumption that betrayal could not happen to you blinded you from seeing earlier warning signs that it might happen.

HFT beliefs instead of LFT beliefs Here, you need to show yourself that while you may 'feel' that you cannot bear the betrayal, having this 'feeling' doesn't prove that you can't put up with it. You would do so to save the life of a child and you could do so for yourself as well, and it is worth it to do so. Why? Because doing so will help you to move on with your life and form other relationships.

Acceptance beliefs as opposed to depreciation beliefs If you hold an other-depreciation belief, you need to show yourself that the person who betrayed your trust is not a bad person. The betrayal is bad, but the person is not. Rather, he or she is a fallible human being capable of acting in a trustworthy way and in an untrustworthy way. This does not mean that you should continue to have a relationship with that person. Rather, it means that you don't have to damn people for their damnable behaviour.

If you hold a life-depreciation belief, you need to show yourself again that while the betrayal was bad, life is not all bad for permitting this betrayal. Life, in truth, is a complex place where trustworthy and untrustworthy acts occur. Reminding yourself of this will help you to move forward and live healthily in this complex and ambiguous world.

You will experience a number of constructive responses if you develop the above set of rational beliefs

When your beliefs about betrayal are rational, your main emotional responses are sorrow, healthy anger and sadness. You remain involved with life, stay in communication with relevant people and feel a desire to express your healthy anger to the person who has betrayed your trust. You tend to think that some men (or women) are to be trusted and others aren't, and when the time is right you think you will develop another relationship and be prepared to risk being betrayed again.

Obstacles to dealing with betrayal-related disturbance and how to address them

In this section, I will briefly list the three main obstacles to dealing with betrayal-related disturbance and show how you can address them.

Obstacle 1

'If I give up my demand about the betrayal happening, there is no point in trusting anyone.'

Response: 'I am more likely to choose to trust someone again once I have given up my demand about betrayal. Indeed, one of the thinking consequences of my unmet demand about betrayal is "I will never trust anyone again."'

Obstacle 2

'I need to hurt the person who hurt me because otherwise he or she will betray someone else in the future.'

Response: 'There are more adaptive and effective ways of communicating my feelings of hurt to someone who has betrayed me than hurting him or her. If I hurt the person in response, it may not be understood why I have done so. Clear communication without hurting the person is more likely to get the message across. Also, if I hurt someone for hurting me, he or she may then hurt me in response and the spiral of hurt will increase rather than decrease.'

Obstacle 3

'If I accept that the person who betrayed me is fallible, I am making excuses for his or her bad behaviour.'

Response: 'Holding that the person who betrayed me is fallible is a fact and is not intended to be an excuse for his or her bad behaviour. I can accept that person as fallible and still hold him or her fully accountable for betraying me, which means not making any excuses for this behaviour.'

How Josie dealt with her betrayal-related disturbance

Josie had been dating Mike for two years and they had just become engaged. It had taken her a long time, but she had learned to trust Mike. Two weeks after getting engaged, she discovered that Mike had been having a year-long affair with Sonya, Josie's best friend. Josie considered that both had betrayed her trust and disturbed herself by believing that the two most trustworthy people in her life (apart from her immediate family members) absolutely should not have betrayed her trust. Believing this, Josie felt terribly hurt and cut both of them out of her life, together with all her other friends, whom she suspected of knowing about the affair. Josie concluded that she would only trust her family and would not make friends or go out with men again.

At the behest of her worried parents, Josie sought counselling a year after the double betrayal. After six months of counselling, Josie had begun the process of moving on: she had got back in touch with some of her old friends and had begun dating. She achieved this by acknowledging the following:

- She is not, nor does she have to be, immune from being betrayed in life. Such betrayal is a possibility that needs to be accepted and borne in mind and incorporated in a world view that indicates that such things can happen to her (see the next section for a discussion of such world views). These beliefs helped Josie to feel sorrow rather than hurt when she thought of what happened between her fiancé and her best friend.
- There is no evidence that all her friends knew about the affair, so she decided to get back in touch with some of them.
- There is also no evidence that all men are untrustworthy and so she began dating again.

World views: simple and complex

When you hold a set of irrational beliefs about unfairness, injustice and betrayal and you experience these adversities, you tend to go from an excessively rosy view of the world to an excessively negative world view. Thus:

- The world is fair. If something unfair happens, as it must not do, it proves that the world is unfair.
- The world is just. If something unjust happens, as it must not do, it proves that the world is unjust.
- People close to me can be trusted. If one of them betrays my trust, as they must not do, it proves that these people are all untrustworthy.

However, when you hold a set of rational beliefs about unfairness, injustice and betrayal and you experience these adversities, you retain a realistic view of the world. Thus:

- The world is comprised of a complex mixture of fairness and unfairness. If something unfair happens I would prefer that it didn't, but it does not have to be the way I want it to be. If an unfairness happens, it does not change my view of the world.
- The world is comprised of a complex mixture of justice and injustice. If something unjust happens I would prefer that it didn't, but it does not have to be the way I want it to be. If an injustice happens, it does not change my view of the world.
- Some people close to me can be trusted and others can't be. If one of them betrays my trust, as I would prefer but do not demand that they not do, it does not change my view of people.

We have now come to the end of the book. I hope that you have found it useful, and that it may have helped you to deal with your own challenges in life and encouraged you to move on from adversity. I would welcome your feedback c/o the publisher.

Index

adversity (A)
actual events 4–5; CBT model 2; inferred events 5; *see also* problems

anger
healthy and unhealthy 7, 8; losing control 68

anxiety
about doing harm 66–7; health 45, 48–54; losing control 68–9; uncertainty and 45; vs concern 7, 8

assertiveness
seeking approval and 85–7

awfulizing beliefs 3, 4; betrayal 110, 111; hardship from loss 41; health anxiety 48, 50; injustice 105, 107; loss 34–5; personal limitations 21–2; uncertainty 57–8; unfairness and 100, 102, 103–4

Beck, Dr Aaron 2
personal domains 32

behaviour
East–West approaches 70–4; negative emotions and 7–8; uncertainty and 55–6, 58; unfairness and 103; *see also* control

beliefs (B)
about personal limitations 19–24; about unfairness 99–104; betrayal 109–13; CBT model 2; control and 64–6; controlling external world 61–3; effect of adversity 5; injustice 105–9; personal limitations 21–2; types of irrational 3; types of rational 3–4; in uncertainty 57–8; uncertainty and 55; worry and 45–6; *see also* awfulizing beliefs; demands; frustration; tolerance; self-acceptance; self-depreciation

betrayal
defining 98; interpretation of 109; using ABC framework 109–13; world views and 113

Cognitive Behaviour Therapy (CBT)
ABC model 2; benefits of 14–16; concept of 1–2; healthy and unhealthy emotions 6–7

consequences (C)
CBT model 2; three aspects of 6–13; *see also* behaviour; emotions; thinking

control
complete loss of 72; defining 59–60; East-West views of 69–72; emotional 68–9; external 60–3; failure and 81–3; helplessness 63; inner 60, 63–6; paradoxical approach 71–2; Serenity Prayer and 59; of thinking 66–8; uncertainty and 72–3; using ABC framework 61, 64–6, 67–8

demands
being looked after 89–94; betrayal 110, 111; health anxiety and 49–50; injustice and 105; personal limitations and 20–1; rigid 3; unfairness and 100, 101–2

denial
loss and 34

depression
bipolar affective disorder 18, 29–30; helplessness 63; vs sadness 7, 8

difference
personal limitations 27–31

disapproval
see rejection and disapproval

Dryden, Windy
Overcoming Shame 24

Ellis, Dr Albert 1
ABC model 2–4

emotions
dependence 89–91; Eastern approach 70; healthy negative 6–7; losing control 68–9; unfairness and 100, 103; unhealthy negative 6–7

envy
   healthy and unhealthy 7, 8
Epictetus 2
expectations
   realistic 15–16; *see also* beliefs

failure
   ABC framework and 74–6, 79–80,
   84–5; causing hardship 83–5;
   competitiveness and 74, 80–1;
   guilt for hurting others 79–80; not
   controlling 81–3; the problem of
   74–6
family
   failing 77–9; inheritance and 18,
   29–30; loss 33; trusting 114
flying, fear of 45, 46
frustration tolerance
   betrayal and 110, 111; health
   anxiety and 48, 50; high 4;
   injustice and 105, 107; loss and 35,
   36–7; low 3; personal limitations
   and 22–3, 25–6; unfairness and
   100, 102

goals
   CBT directed towards 15
   in uncertainty 55, 57
grief
   see loss
guilt feelings
   control and 71; deserved loss
   40–1; for failure 79–80; vs remorse
   7, 8

hardship
   caused by failure 83–5; dealing
   with 42–4
health anxiety 45
   challenging beliefs 49–52;
   constructive behaviours 53–4;
   probability quadrants 51–3;
   uncertainty and 48–9
home and place, loss of 33
hurt vs sorrow 7, 8

inferences
   rejection from loss 38–9
injustice
   defining 98; interpreting 104;

using ABC framework 105–9; world
   views and 113

jealousy
   betrayal and 113–14; healthy and
   unhealthy 7, 8

loss
   deserving 40–1; elements and
   kinds 32–3; hardship from 41–4; as
   rejection 38–40; rigid beliefs about
   33–7

mental abilities
   personal limitations 19

National Association for Loss and
   Grief 33

obsessive–compulsive disorder (OCD)
   uncertainty and 45, 46–8
Overcoming Shame (Dryden) 24

panic
   fear of losing control 72
Pauling, Linus 74, 80–1
personal limitations
   being different 27–31; ideals and
   24–5; irrational beliefs about
   19–27; types of 17–19
personality 18
phrenophobia 72
physical abilities
   loss 33; personal limitations 19
preferences, non-dogmatic 4
problems
   CBT focus on 14; *see also* control;
   loss; personal limitations; rejection
   and disapproval; uncertainty;
   unfairness

Rational Emotive Behaviour Therapy
   (REBT) 1, 2; healthy and unhealthy
   emotions 6–7; inferences 38
rejection and disapproval
   ABC framework and 87–92;
   guidelines for dealing with 92–4;
   issues of 86; loss and 38–40;
   overestimating approval need 94–7
Robinson, Smokey 28

self-acceptance 4
  disapproval and rejection 94–7;
  personal limitations 30–1;
  unfairness and 102
self-depreciation 3
  betrayal and 110, 111; hardship
  from loss 41–2; injustice 105, 107;
  loss 35, 37; personal limitations
  23–4; unfairness and 100, 102
self-help
  learning CBT 15
  see also under individual problems
self-reliance 92–4
Serenity Prayer 59, 63
shame
  control of thinking 67–8; failure
  and 77–9; vs disappointment 7, 8
social relations
  failing your group 77–9; ideals and
  24–5; loss 33; mind-reading others
  11
Stoicism 2

temperament 19
thinking
  all-or-none 9; always/never 11;
  anticipation 11; balanced 11, 12;
  distorted vs realistic 8–13; Eastern
  approach to 70; emotional 13;
  generalizing 10; losing control

of 66–8; magnification 12; mind-
reading 11; minimization 12;
multi-category 9; negative 9,
10; personalization 13; realistic
perspectives 12, 13; unfairness and
103
tolerance
  of difference 27–31; wise rabbi
  story 42–3; see also self-
  acceptance

uncertainty
  control and 72–3; fear of flying
  45, 46; health anxiety 48–9;
  how it disturbs 45–6; obsessive–
  compulsive disorder 46–8; using
  the ABC framework 54–8
unfairness
  challenging irrational beliefs
  99–104; defining unfairness 98;
  interpreting 98–9; loss and 40–1;
  personal limitations and 26–7;
  world views and 113; see also
  betrayal; injustice

work and employment
  loss 33
worry 45–6

Young, Howard 37